PASSIVE INCOME IDEAS 2020

Discover the Best Ways to Make Money Today! Amazon FBA, Social Media Marketing, Influencer Marketing, E-Commerce, Dropshipping, Blogging, Trading, Self-Publishing, etc...

BY
Blake Davis

TABLE OF CONTENTS

INTRODUCTION.. 3

CHAPTER 1 HOW TO MAKE MONEY OFF A
BLOG WITH THE RIGHT MESSAGES........................ 8

CHAPTER 2 MARKETING: LEVERAGE THE
POWER OF SOCIAL MEDIA 13

CHAPTER 3 HOW TO GENERATE PASSIVE
INCOME THROUGH INFLUENCER.......................... 17

CHAPTER 4 HOW TO DO DROP SHIPPING AND
SUCCEED IN THE SHORTEST POSSIBLE TIME 40

CHAPTER 5 AMAZON FBA 64

CHAPTER 6 AFFILIATE MARKETING?.................. 73

CHAPTER 7 REAL ESTATE 87

CHAPTER 8 HOW TO MAKE MONEY WITH A
PODCAST.. 98

CHAPTER 9 NETWORK MARKETING.................... 115

CHAPTER 10 KINDLE PUBLISHING 125

CHAPTER 11 DEVELOP YOUR APP 136

CHAPTER 12 HOW TO MAKE MONEY ON
YOUTUBE? 145

CHAPTER 13 PASSIVE INCOME WITH P2P
LOANS.. 149

CHAPTER 14 TRADING... 157

Introduction

No one needs to work 50 or more hours, seven days for long. If you do, you're insane. If you don't, you better start learning a few things about passive income. It's the retirement plan of intelligent people. In case you maintain a business or need to keep a company, with the end goal to have the opportunity in life you long for you need to start thinking of some passive income ideas to enable you to earn increasingly and work less.

It is an incredible inclination when you can require some serious energy off at whatever point you need to, without stressing over what will happen to your business.

As a business person, there is always going to be a limit on the amount you can earn except if you can make money without being engaged explicitly with the work. You're not rich except if you can make money in your rest.

Passive income ideas enable a business visionary to earn income without requiring your immediate contribution — for instance; sovereignties on an innovative piece (music, book, creation, and so forth), owning property, offers, and network marketing.

There are numerous ways to earn a passive income, some less demanding than others. The most excellent ways are to purchase a venture property or put resources into offers, yet these expect you to have the money in any case. The best passive income ideas are the ones that require little startup expenses; however, they still, offer to compensate compensation whenever executed well.

There is no denying we are in the age of the web, and all things considered, there are many open doors online to earn a passive income. Activities like Google AdSense enable people to receive money from making prominent content. There are additionally many affiliate programs that will allow you to earn a rate when people click through from your site and purchase an item; Amazon is notable for this. If you can make content online that people need to see, there are numerous ways to make a benefit out of it.

At that point, there is network marketing; there are a large number of old and new network marketing organizations going back and forth constantly. Customarily, the trick shame has always been appended to network marketing and sometimes in light of current circumstances, however, there are numerous legitimate organizations engaged with this kind of marketing nowadays, and there is some genuine money to be made for people that can do it well.

We have just talked around a couple of the passive income ideas that are out there; there are a large number of ways to earn the remaining income. It might originate from rehashed deals or new clients, and it might require a tad bit of your time or zero; however, the key is that you are making money off of other people's work or no work, instead of by your own.

Applying It

There is no time like the present to start thinking about how to incorporate this kind of thinking in your business. You have to ask yourself; would you be able to make an item that people will purchase again and again? Would you be able to connect with others to offer your piece? How might you make money off crafted by others?

The sooner you answer these inquiries, the sooner you'll have money related and individual flexibility. Start thinking about some passive income ideas that will enable your business to wind up less time expanding and start living your fantasies while you keep on earning income.

Numerous people think about whether there are passive income ideas accessible, which could transform a customary blog into a genuine way to make money. Shockingly, the appropriate response is yes - a vast number of bloggers are getting some answers concerning the passive income streams they could be utilized further bolstering their advantage. Loads of people have gotten on board the temporary blogging fad. Who wouldn't like to wind up a distributed author with many faithful fans?

When we discovered that writing business or individual weblogs could make us money, we as a whole needed to get in on it. A couple of passive income ideas, a great blog (and they exist on about each subject), and the adoration for writing can be genuine benefit makers. Passive income streams are wherever for people who realize how to utilize them legitimately.

In any case, the world is loaded with scholars who aren't profiting. The clients are making the most and utilizing their income ideas minus all potential limitations are energetic about what they do. Nobody needs to peruse content that even the essayist had no enthusiasm for. An extremely devoted after of all-around pointed guests is essential to make the large portion of the income streams accessible. Nobody ought to overlook that the readers are the place the money originates from. Disregarding the readers implies losing the possibility of a decent benefit.

The clients destined to bomb, regardless of whether they have excellent passive income ideas, are the ones who blog on everything without exception. It may appear to be bizarre since numerous people would imagine that these blogs would pull in more readers. In any case, readers need blogs to be about only a specific something. Sites with arbitrary themes aren't as prone to assemble a decent gathering of people as sites with a substantial core interest.

Genuinely fruitful bloggers will create something their readers need. These blogs additionally have very much focused on publicizing that will draw in that gathering of people. That is the reason that focused activity is so valuable. People who need to get all that they can out of blogging will assemble solid content and income streams that aren't anything but trying to disturb. The final product will be a genuinely fantastic dimension of money streaming in - effortlessly and with minimal extra work.

CHAPTER 1

HOW TO MAKE MONEY OFF A BLOG WITH THE RIGHT MESSAGES

We regularly hear the prosaism, "what leaves your mouth is an impression of your identity and character." True enough, the messages you use to pass on your considerations and to persuade others to acknowledge your position play a somewhat primary point for your success. The capacity to make and convey messages that impact understudies, workers, markets, and different types of audiences may appear to be an ability that a few people have while others don't. In this digital age, with the presentation of blogging, realizing how to express one's contemplations can be monetarily gainful for grown-ups as well as for children who need to learn how to make money off a blog.

Regardless of whether you are beginning on a blog or recording an open discourse or communicating an honest thought, characterizing your destinations is imperative. Your message has a more noteworthy shot of success on the off chance that you know from the begin what you anticipate accomplish with it. It is safe to say that you are essentially blogging for the sake of entertainment? Is it true that you are attempting to set up yourself as a specialist in your field? Is it true that you are endeavoring to advance your business? Your words must affect, must be correct and reliable, and should contact people. Probably the best discourses are more intuitive than balanced. You realize your message changes when it addresses people's very own encounters.

Another perspective to consider is the amount you know your audience. Think about what your specific audience would need to hear. Is it accurate to say that they are longing for new data or experiences? What issue do they plan to fathom? Give them what they need and need. Your content ought to imitate the desires of your audience. For instance, how to make money off a blog would be decidedly not quite the same as what you would regularly have with business experts, regarding your content and approach. Solicit yourself what kind from the message is this specific audience prepared to hear? Never feel wrong when you foresee any presumptions or misunderstandings that your audience may land at. Thus, it is fundamental that your blogs welcome the audience and welcomes them to participate in a two-manner discussion. By doing this, not exclusively will it demonstrate your audience that you esteem them. However, it will fuel the exchange. It will make them see the amount you value them by including them and remembering them through significant two-route discussions, rather than merely having a restricted monolog.

In like manner, being steady enables you to live up to your audience's desires. Having a key message helps your audience in holding data and should assist in accomplishing that consistency. While you might be enticed to discover engaging approaches to state things, this frequently makes your audience recognize trouble in understanding your real significance. Decide the core of your message and realize how best to build and convey it. Infuse your identity into your words and adjust a positive tone to your conveyance; at that point, remain steady with that condition all through.

In conclusion, keep your messages short. There are a few people that basically can't ingest excessively data at a time. As is commonly said, don't give people more than what they can process. Utilizing short, explanatory sentences will add immediacy and clarity to your message.

Building blogs to interest a particular audience isn't an easy procedure. In any case, you should likewise recall that the message and how it is being conveyed is similarly as vital. On the off chance that you have examined your specific audience painstakingly, you ought to have a quick thought of how these people take data in and start to process it. When you have begun creating your messages, test them. You may solicit some from your companions or families to be your intended interest group and tune in to your notes, and after that, give you criticism.

As should be obvious, having extremely unusual content is only one of the numerous routes on the best way to make money off a blog. Blogging implies getting the chance to discuss your most loved things, composing imaginatively, and in particular, profiting. It takes time, involvement, and concentrates on making a luring blog. Your physical market is continually changing, so it just makes sense to keep things liquid. Endeavor to check out you and see what pulls you in.

Instructions to Make Money at Home - Why Online Opportunities Are Goldmine to Be Tapped.

If you are considering how to make money at home, going online is undoubtedly the best approach. It is a goldmine, not so much tapped by numerous people. If you need to earn money at home, you ought not to pass up a great opportunity the online opportunities effectively gotten to through the internet.

In this busy current society that we are in now, a great many people are busy with their timetable, however not earning enough. In the event that you have an occupation, regardless of whether you put in 24 hours working, you will in any case not gain to such an extent and will understand that when coming to retirement, you don't have much money left in your pocket since all were spend to see through the high living expense.

If you are an understudy, you are so busy with your investigations and extra activities that you scarcely discover enough time for different things. Some may even need to work low maintenance to help themselves through their training, which could be a terrible impact on their investigations because of less time spend on their homework.

Concerning people who have effectively resigned, they may have annuities to see them through their life. In any case, the vast majority who left needed extra money to have an actual existence that they can surrender serenely. Tragically they couldn't work any longer, as a large portion of the companies will dismiss them on account of the age. For a few, they may not have annuities to enable them to resign and don't have work to help them. The central arrangement presently is to earn money at home. This is by benefiting the opportunities online.

Regardless of whether you are an understudy who doesn't have room schedule-wise to do extra activities or a retiree who nobody need to utilize you In the event that you are discovering how to make money at home, you would now be able to take advantage of the a great many opportunities accessible online to earn extra income from the solace of your home. All you need is a PC with a quick internet association.

If you search on the internet, you can discover approaches to make money online. You can make money taking studies, as companies will reward you the time for topping off overview structures to get criticism for their items or administrations. You can earn money at home with information passage occupations that incorporate arranging the companies' databases, planning of the spreadsheet, et cetera. In any case, you need to be mindful of making you work with real companies, as there are numerous tricks out there in the market.

CHAPTER 2

MARKETING: LEVERAGE THE POWER OF SOCIAL MEDIA

Presently your store is ready for action, next you need to tell people about your new business! Social media can be an incredible marketing device once you realize how to utilize it.

Facebook Adverts

To run a Facebook Ad crusade, you will initially need to set up an FB page for your business and run two adverts; one to publicize your Facebook page and one to connect back to your store.

Set a financial plan of $6 — $10 multi-day, relying upon the amount you will spend; however, ensure you place a final spending plan of £50 — $100 altogether.

Concerning your FB page, present relevant content on the specialty you are selling in, for example, if you are selling fitness products, current articles related to fitness to keep your gathering of people locked in.

The point of your Facebook page is to draw in intrigue, so

stay with connecting with, fascinating, and even interesting substance as long as it is identified with the specialty your product is selling in.

Instagram Marketing

Keep in mind the Instagram example I referenced before? Well, now you can contact the favorite Instagram influencers yourself and inquire as to whether they will advance your products for you.

Uncovered as a top priority that the bigger after the influencer has, the more they will anticipate that you will pay, the littler and less important influencers may even do a few advancements for nothing to kick them off yet I depend on free promotions as a technique.

Check what number of adherents the influencer has an offer to pay $25 — $50 to influencers who have 100,000–250,000 supporters.

You can even contact Instagrammers with under 100,0000 adherents (i.e., 60,000– 90,000) yet don't offer more than $25 for advancements from them.

When you have discovered your picked Instagrammer, send them a DM, and get arranging!

Marketing: Customer Targeting

While targeting your customers, it is best to be particular; this goes for FB advertisements and social media pages.

If you are selling fitness watches, target people who are dynamic and heading off to the exercise center routinely, If that you are selling diet formulas, target people who are attempting to get more fit.

When running your adverts, it regards pick huge urban areas (for example, Los Angeles and New York on the off chance that you are targeting US customers and London or Birmingham on the off chance that you are targeting UK based customers).

Wrapping Up

So to entirety everything up:

· Research potential products utilizing Amazon and rundown 20 of your most loved products

· Fabricate your online store with Shopify

· Utilize the Oberlo plugin or source products utilizing Alibaba.

· Setup your payment processor

· Market your store utilizing Facebook and Instagram.

· At long last keep in mind to reinvest your benefits, as your business develops, the request will develop so you need to return your cash to your business to take into account the convergence of new customers.

While the home industry used to be slightly skeptical and could only be implemented for the fewest people without prepayment and risks, today, everyone has the chance of a passive income on the internet. Social networks and their performance have created entirely new possibilities and show how you can earn cash with your hobby and increase your budget without undue burden.

CHAPTER 3

HOW TO GENERATE PASSIVE INCOME THROUGH INFLUENCER

Have you ever felt influenced to perform a specific action? Surely it has all happened to us that we do something just because we see that someone else does it. This is not necessarily a bad thing, and since we are born, we do everything by imitation: talking, dressing, going to the bathroom, among many other things.

The first influencers are our parents, we all want to do like them until time passes and we unconsciously identify personalities that attract us and decide to imitate some of them. These people who inspire us to imitate them are called influencers, and as always, brands, identifying areas of opportunity, take advantage of this situation to promote their service or product through them, helped by social networks in trend.

The media change and the way we interact with brands and reach the purchase decision is not the same as ten years ago.

Have you noticed that most of your favorite vloggers recommend products, services, or applications in your videos?

17

Today the competition is quite fierce, that is why you have to know how to take advantage of what is fashionable to promote your brand.

Now the brands are focused on advertising through the famous influencers. It is not enough to show a commercial or advertise your product in print or old media. Nowadays, it is essential to cover all possible means for your brand to be recognized; one of these media is YouTube.

Being an influencer means reaching many people, both from your country and from other places, are those people who, through their opinion, can influence a niche market, so the name. It is here where advertising can take advantage.

That's why we can see Yuya recommending her favorite makeup brands, or Heyitspriscila showing her favorite outfits of branded clothes.

It should be noted that there are different types of advertising that influencers apply on YouTube:

- **Recommendations/opinions:** There are YouTubers who, as such, buy a product, turn on their camera and give their advice about it, or who have had a good experience with a service.

- **Commercial:** This is an excellent example of how a brand can hire an influencer and promote its product to reach a large market.

- **Challenges:** In addition to giving opinions about products, there are also the "challenges," for example, the Bubble challenge where the brand sent a box with the product to several YouTubers to make creative challenges with it. Many times the brand also asks influencers to challenge each other so that there are more videos and more people watch them.

- **Promote movies:** A more recent example is when the movie "Suicide Squad" came out, and Cinepolis invited several YouTubers to the premiere, this pulled more audiences. There is also the type of advertising where they are asked to make a short film or go to a conviviality to promote the movie.

The power that influencers have today is shocking, and it makes the public trustworthy to buy the product or try the service just by listening to it from their favorite YouTuber, in addition to being able to reach a broad audience.

How To Make Money On Instagram Being An Influencer

Without a doubt, Instagram has become the most used social network for young people and adults. Brands have also seen the incredible potential of this application to promote their products but not in any way but through the so-called influencers, who are paid for their publications. But is it possible to make money while being an influencer? How to make money on Instagram? How to be an influencer? How many followers do you have to have on Instagram to make money?

Admittedly, these questions are hanging around your head...

If you would also like to become an influencer and want to earn money while using this application, so, keep reading this chapter, I'll tell you how to be an influencer and make money.

Before getting deep into the subject...

What is Instagram?

Instagram is an application that allows you to upload photos and videos by adding filters and frames and share them with friends either on the same social network or on others such as Facebook, Twitter, and Tumblr.

This application came to light in October 2010, and at first, it was only available for iPhone, today you can also find it on Android.

In December of the same year, just three months later, one million people already used it. This caught the attention of Mark Zuckerberg, who announced in April 2012 that Instagram had been bought by Facebook, for nothing more and nothing less than a billion dollars.

And what is an influencer?

An influencer is a person who has achieved some credibility on some subject and can influence other people when making decisions.

In recent years, Instagram has become the most active social network for influencers, who have taken advantage of their potential to become attractive characters for brands.

Why has Instagram become a tool to earn money?

As I said above, Instagram is one of the most used social networks today. Every day millions of people use this application, so for brands, it is a showcase open to everyone, 24 hours a day, and 365 days a year.

These are the essential Instagram statistics you should know if you are thinking about being an influencer (2019 data):

- It has more than 900 million active users every day. The number of users is vital so that this social network has become a channel for business with such success.

- Twenty-five million companies have an Instagram profile.

- Brands have created 70% of hashtags on Instagram.

21

- 80% of Instagram users follow at least one brand or company.

- Every day, more than 300 million users consult the profile of a company. Two out of every three people who visit a brand's profile are people who don't follow them.

- 92% of users considered more reliable the opinion of other consumers before brand advertising.

The main conclusion I draw from this data is that: we love this application. We like to be active users and consume content, and brands know it very well. Also, as in the day to day, if someone tells us about a product or service that they liked, we trust more.

How many followers do you have to have on Instagram to earn money?

The great question!

The first thing you have thought about is that you need a lot of followers to be able to earn money as an influencer.

The truth is that it is not always the case; it depends on the area in which you want to stand out. There are people who, despite having few followers, produce a more significant impact than celebrities and are sought by some brands. These people are known as micro-influencer.

However, some themes are more crowded than others,

and therefore, the opportunities to stand out among leading personalities will be lower, so your interactions with followers will also be reduced. The result will be that your profile will not draw attention to brands.

So, to answer the question, how many followers do you have to have on Instagram to make money? It is said that in general, for an influencer to start making money on Instagram, he must have at least 10,000 followers.

And what influence are you?

According to the First Micro-influencers Study prepared by SocialPubli, influencers can be categorized according to the number of followers on Instagram:

- Nano influencers: <1,000 followers

- Micro-influencers: <10,000 followers

- Macro influencers: <100,000 followers

- Mega influencers: <1 MM followers

- Top: 1 MM + followers

According to this classification, the vast majority are nano influencers. Our leading followers are our relatives, close friends, and some acquaintances. We exert some influence on them when we talk about something we liked. However, this is not going to make us money on Instagram.

However, as a micro-influencer, you may start earning money from some brands by talking about them. But in the beginning, you will have to settle free products. Some brands will compensate you with gifts when you talk about them if you are a micro-influencer.

But without a doubt, a macro influencer will make money by promoting products or services on his Instagram account.

So, according to this study, there is no exact figure that assures you that you will earn money with this application. If you have a few followers, you will not go far. The study also tells us that you can start earning with less than 10,000 followers. But, as I said to you before, it depends on the competence of the area in which you want to stand out.

My advice is that instead of just looking at the number of followers, you focus on the quality and frequency of your content.

How much money can influencers earn on Instagram?

According to this BBC article, an influencer who has at least 10,000 followers on his Instagram account, can start "earning something." Although it is considered a low-level influencer, you can charge $ 130 for a publication.

In the case of influencers with 30 thousand followers, earnings per publication (for fashion or beauty brands) increase, exceeding $ 970.

If we talk about the Mega or Top influencer, these gains are more significant, even reaching six figures!

But in addition to the number of followers, the earnings vary depending on the country of residence, the product or service being promoted, and the brand.

So, would you like to make money on Instagram?

Once you have reached a significant number of followers (the more, the better), these are some ways to generate money with your account.

1. ***Post sponsored posts***

Sponsored content is the form most used by influencers and the primary way to generate revenue. This method is also used to monetize blogs.

You can get paid for posting sponsored content on your Instagram account, even if you don't have millions of followers.

How?

Some platforms put brands in contact with influencers. Many of them accept profiles with a few thousand followers.

Attention! If you think that by buying followers, you will get the brands to contact you, you are wrong. Brands are interested in the interaction of your followers, that they are active and that you notice that you exert some influence on them. When an account has purchased followers, it is easy to realize: no comments, few likes, poor visibility of your stories, etc.

The publication of sponsored content can be a photo, several photos, a video, one or several stories, or putting a link to the website of the brand or its products. The more they ask you, the more you can win.

1. *Promote affiliate products*

This way of monetizing your profile is the promotion of third-party products or services. You will get a commission every time someone buys it.

To make money on Instagram with affiliate products, the first thing you have to do is find products or services that are of interest to your audience and that are related to the content you share on your profile.

You can continue sharing your photos or videos as you usually do. And from time to time, recommend a product using your affiliate link. Thus, every time a sale is registered, you will receive a commission.

1. *Be a brand ambassador*

For some brands, it is essential to maintain a long-term relationship with an influencer, and even more so if you have thousands of followers. That is why some companies are willing to pay an influencer to be the image of their brand.

In these cases, your tasks will go beyond an Instagram post. They will invite you to events, new product launches. Can you imagine this? Well, for that, you will have to reach several hundred thousand followers.

1. *Sell your photographs*

This is another way to make money online, although it does not have to do directly with this application, but with the quality of photos, you take and share.

The photographs that you have uploaded to your Instagram account can be sold to image banks and earn money when a company purchases them.

And for this, you do not have to have a minimum number of followers; it is merely necessary that your photos are of good quality.

There are different platforms wherein a few minutes you can register and upload the photos you want to sell. It is an excellent option to generate income passively.

1. *Promote your products or services*

If big brands use Instagram to promote their products, you can also do the same.

With your content, you can show your skills and

professionalism, and thus gain credibility and closeness with your followers, who will be more willing to buy something from you.

I have left this idea in the end because although you are not going to generate money directly, it is an excellent way to create an active and faithful audience. This will increase the sale of your products.

The five influencers who earn more money on Instagram

These five people make the most money for each post on Instagram:

1. Kylie Jenner. One hundred twenty-one million followers, 1 million dollars per post.

2. Selena Gomez. 144.4 million Followers, 800 thousand dollars per post.

3. Cristiano Ronaldo. One hundred forty-eight million followers, 750 thousand dollars per post.

4. Kim Kardashian West. 121.7 million Followers, 720 thousand dollars per post.

5. Beyoncé Knowles. 121.3 million Followers, 700 thousand dollars per post.

Ten practical tips to become an influencer and earn money on Instagram:

1. Become an app expert. Learn to use Instagram and take advantage of all its features.

2. Motivate your followers. Brands are more willing to pay an influencer if they see that their audience is active.

3. Upload good quality photos. It is no use uploading 1 picture every 15 minutes if they are out of focus, moved, or dark. The quality of the photos you share is the key.

4. Learn to edit photographs and get results like celebrities.

5. Do not go over with the sponsored content. Your followers will not like that your content is always to promote a product. In the same way, your audience will not see with good eyes that promotions products that do not correspond to the rest of your content.

6. Be constant. If you want to become a real influencer and earn money on Instagram, you must post frequently. If you follow some influencer, you will see that their presence in social networks is constant.

7. Create your media kit and show yourself as a professional. A media kit is a document where you summarize and attract all your potential to

potential advertisers, through data.

8. Study the brands. Do not assume that all brands in your segment are good options for your profile. Research, study and choose the most exciting and related companies to you and your content.

9. Register on influencers platforms. If you are determined, do not wait any longer. Search and choose the best influencer platform for you (or the one you like) and register.

10. Contact the brands. If you already have a significant number of active followers and add value to your profile, which makes you different from others. So, don't sit around, waiting for brands to knock on your door. Contact directly, present your media kit, and propose a collaboration.

Affiliate Marketing vs. Influencer Marketing

Affiliate marketing vs. Influencer marketing. What type of marketing is best suited for the current objectives of your company? Affiliate marketing and Influencer marketing are two disciplines that use promoters to suggest or promote products.

Also, with the two, you get an extraordinary value regarding the return on investment. But which one should you choose for your strategy? Affiliate marketing vs.

Influencer marketing, a decision that will affect your online marketing strategies.

Differences in affiliate marketing vs. influencer marketing

Influencer marketing refers to the process of identifying key individuals who have a strong presence in networks and use their influence on followers or subscribers to promote a product or service.

Influencers can be bloggers, journalists, authors, consultants, analysts, etc. Of course, the most valuable influencers usually have:

- A strong influence on potential customers.

- A vital audience reaches on your website and an essential social media presence.

- The ability to convey a strong brand affinity.

- Credibility and trust with your audience as experts in a given topic.

Influencers can help brands strengthen and increase their awareness and affinity with the brand because their followers trust their recommendations.

In marketing affiliation, meanwhile, a company partners with affiliates (bloggers, publishers, companies, organizations, etc.) to promote their brand.

In both cases, they are used for the same purpose, but then, to what extent are they different, when to use one or the other? These are five factors that you must take into account when making a decision:

1. - Study your target audience

It is one of the essential aspects to decide between affiliate marketing vs. influencer marketing. Affiliates can help bring your articles to your ideal audience, with direct links to your company's products or services.

However, if your goal is to publicize a product through recommendations, you will have to think about customizing your sale with influencers.

2. - New ways of marketing

Years ago, affiliate marketing had just begun. Now, the software allows companies to go further than ever. In the same way that marketing with influencers has flourished thanks to social networks.

Knowing the right time to use each one is to opt for a long-term option. Affiliate marketing may be the right strategy for a specific campaign while betting on influencers will be ideal at another time.

3. - Differentiated costs

Affiliates are paid a portion of the proceeds from the sale that they have helped generate from their website, a commission for the sale. This compensation structure makes affiliate marketing one of the most profitable strategies.

On the contrary, with Influencer marketing, the influencer is paid a flat rate depending, among other factors, on the number of followers he has to promote the brand. Also, the influencer can obtain products free in exchange for his promotion.

Affiliate programs are primarily designed to get new customers and, therefore, increase revenue. Influencer marketing tends to focus more on brand awareness to achieve the same end.

4. - Measurement and monitoring

Influencer marketing uses the site of influencer and social analysis to track and measure advertising focused on the brand. This includes metrics such as the following:

- Total audience: Subscribers, social followers, blog traffic, website visits.

- Social Engagement: Visits, I like you, clicks on links, comments, social sentiment.

- Social Sharing: Participations.

- Subscriptions to newsletters.

- New followers in the different social media spaces of the brand.

Affiliate marketing uses tracking cookies and a pixel placed on the brand's site to track and measure advertising focused on the response. These metrics are often more tangible and can lead to a more reliable ROI calculation for the brand. This includes:

- Registrations, email signatures, raffle tickets.

- Sales, orders, subscriptions.

- Conversion Rate

- New customer Vs. recurring customer.

- Average order value.

- Cost per acquisition (CPA).

- Customer lifetime value (CLV).

5. - Problems of both disciplines

However, both affiliate marketing and influencer marketing also have to face several disadvantages, including:

A. - Incentives

The Federal Trade Commission (FTC), the agency that applies the laws of truth in advertising of the USA, has begun to take active measures against brands that encourage bloggers, publishers, or those who publish about their products and services and do not make public those incentives.

In the Influencer marketing model, in many cases, the compensation they receive from brands to promote their products is also not revealed.

Another problem for brands that work with influencers is to make sure they work correctly for their compensation. A factor that equally affects the choice between affiliate marketing and influencer marketing.

B. - Rules

Most influential unaffiliated people do not know the basic rules for disclosure, do not understand them, or do not care.

In affiliate marketing, there is a much more structured administration and supervision process to verify that affiliates include a publication disclosure. And in a well-managed program, there are affiliate program managers to enforce what they do.

For example, if an affiliate does not systematically disclose that they will receive a commission if their readers purchase through their site, then the affiliate program administrator can remove them from the program.

That said, Google has recently begun to take intense action against publishers, influencers, and affiliates by requiring them to ensure that each link to a provider is labeled "no follow" in their HTML code and that each relationship with a brand is clear. Something that affects the relationship between affiliation marketing and influencer marketing.

Why online marketing strategy to bet

Have you already decided which option you are going to bet on? The following eight factors will help you make the right choice about affiliate marketing vs. influencer marketing:

1. - Production expenses

For digital media that bet on affiliate marketing as a strategy, you have to know that your production expenses tend to zero. Neither program nor create the product. All this is at the cost of the producing brand. All they have to do is join the corresponding affiliate marketing platform and put the link code on the website where the product is sold.

Therefore, they will receive a code to insert it in the particular URLs, and the sales that are obtained will appear on the platform with which they work. Thus, each online media can access their personalized commission.

In the case of influencers, promotions work together. And it is the brand with the influencer that pacts the price of the different actions to be performed. Production costs will depend on the type of influencer you hire for your campaign.

2. - *Variety of products*

In both cases, there is a wide variety of products to promote, although usually, the influencers move in a more specific niche, which is generally related to gastronomy, fashion, or sports. Especially when it comes to broad-spectrum influencers and not so many micro-influencers.

3. - *There is no after-sales service*

The company, in both cases, will be responsible for the after-sales service. In some cases, the purchase may appear in the affiliate cart, but in the end, the seller's URL always appears. This is one of the similarities of affiliate marketing vs. influencer marketing.

Both disciplines rely on people or other people's means to publicize the products, but there is no previous product purchase. And the after-sales service is, of course, the advertiser brand itself.

4. - *Everyone wins, the company, the client and the affiliate or influencer*

A relationship allows all parties to gain in some way:

- The advertising brand gets new customers and sales.

- The client more easily finds what he is looking for.

- The intermediary receives the appropriate compensation taking advantage of its commercial potential.

5. - Contract

Substantial differences do occur in this aspect. In the case of affiliates, there is usually no specific contract, although the use of a platform results in a series of actions to be performed. For their part, most influencers are already working with a contract.

6. - Passive income

Another significant difference in the choice of affiliate marketing vs. influencer marketing. For the affiliate, it is a passive income. For the influencer, it is a paid job.

7. - Ideal for advertising digital products

If you work with digital products, these two digital marketing disciplines are potentially useful. You could say that it is the update of the commercial that always sold with catalogs and the telephone. Technological advances are what has led to this new way of selling.

8. - Differences in conversion rates

Since the influencers already have loyal followers, the conversion ratio will be better and faster; however, for this, they must have a real and faithful community. Something that in some cases of online media, can lead to reasonable conversion rates. But never so tall.

However, in the relationship marketing affiliation vs. influencer marketing, it is necessary to have the appropriate media and influencers for the strategy to be effective.

CHAPTER 4

HOW TO DO DROP SHIPPING AND SUCCEED IN THE SHORTEST POSSIBLE TIME

Do you need to know how to do Dropshipping?

In this chapter, I want to tell you how to do Dropshipping effectively and profitably.

If you want to have a business online and want to create a source of semi-automatic passive income, it is necessary to tell you about How to Do Dropshipping correctly.

But first let's start at the beginning:

What is dropshipping?

Dropshipping is a logistics technique, which is mainly used in electronic commerce. It is also known as a "Product Brokerage" business model between a supplier and a seller, towards the end customer.

If we divide the word in two, we have: "drop" and "shipping," where "Drop" can mean: drop, drop, drop, launch, etc... while Shipping means "shipping."

Starting from the literal origin of the word, we find that

Drop shipping refers to a technique of "launching, dropping or dropping shipments."

In English, the term Dropshipping has a mental image related to those shipments that are released from the air, with a kind of parachute, which takes them gently from the sky to their destination. This air shipment is also known as "airmail." Although over time, the concept was adapted more to be a modality of assortment and logistics of products in general.

So far, everything is clear?

Okay, now let's explain the "product intermediation" part.

Dropshipping is also a technique for doing business with various product suppliers, through negotiations with them to obtain exciting discounts on the purchase of their products, in exchange for promoting and selling the products of these suppliers on our website and / o Online Store.

It is a technique so popular for doing business online that even Amazon, Walmart, eBay, Best Buy, Sears, and other large online stores or marketplaces even Department Stores use it to fill their customers' orders more efficiently, with minimal risk.

Well, to know how to do Dropshipping, we need to understand the flow of electronic commerce in a general way.

The dropshipping model works as follows (usually):

- You promote the products of suppliers who know and use the Dropshipping model in your Online Store.

- Potential customers visit your Online Store and buy some of these products from your Website.

- Customers pay you for the requested product, directly in your Online Store, and you receive money from your customer.

- With your Client's money in your possession, you (by many available methods) order the product that your client ordered on your Supplier's website (or place an order in some other way)

- You deliver the shipping details of your client to your supplier (that is, you tell him where to send the product, which will be to your client's address)

- Your supplier confirms the order details and is ready to stock and ship the order directly, without you buying or storing inventory.

- Your customer receives your product through the shipping methods of your supplier.

- Your customer is satisfied with their purchase.

- You get a profit for each sale, by subtracting what

the product costs you with your supplier and what you charged the customer in your Online Store.

Now you know what Dropshipping is and how it works?

This business or logistics model, part of the idea of wanting to understand electronic commerce better and its details to have a profitable business minimizing risk, minimizing investment, and offering a more sustainable way to suppliers and vendors who want to have access to the right products at excellent prices. But that does not want (or cannot) make significant investments in inventory in advance.

To know how to do Dropshipping correctly, we already saw some basic concepts, and we already understood a little the general flow of transactions in an Online Store.

Now let's explain the details of Dropshipping.

Advantages of Dropshipping

If you learn how to do Dropshipping correctly, you can benefit a lot (and earn money) with these advantages:

1. You don't need to buy inventory or store it.

Dropshipping is so noble that it allows you to make a direct negotiation with many suppliers, who will offer you discounts in exchange for being them who store and send the products to your customers. This means that you should not buy inventory in advance and perhaps a risk that those products you bought with your money and effort, do not sell and take up space in your home, or worse, in a rented warehouse that only causes you expenses, but not return from the investment.

With dropshipping, suppliers agree to give you wholesale discounts for their entire product catalog, without asking you for any minimum purchase. This means that you can use the Dropshipping model by buying from ONE piece.

2. Profit margins are usually attractive.

To learn dropshipping and how it works, we need to talk about profit margins and why doing dropshipping is usually very attractive, even if this business is your first attempt to create a flow of additional passive income.

As you have access to wholesale discounts with suppliers that use this technique, it is widespread to hear that you can reach discounts ranging from 20% to an exciting (and lucrative) 50% discount for certain low demand products.

It means that if you sell tennis shoes (or sneakers) for USD 150, they may cost you 20-50% less when you buy them directly with your supplier.

That is to say that for each sale, and you can earn up to $ 75USD (depending on the product and supplier, obviously). It should be mentioned that to do dropshipping, you do not need much experience, but a lot of perseverance, but we will talk about the considerations of this method later.

3. *You do not require significant investments and have minimal risk.*

The Dropshipping model implies that you have an Online Store, or that you must create and maintain one. This means that there is some investment associated with starting a Dropshipping business, although it is much less and less risky than building a business in your community, in a physical establishment, for apparent reasons.

Creating your Store in a physical establishment implies some details:

1. You should investigate very thoroughly the area in which you want to establish the location of your Store if you're going to succeed.

2. You must make a significant investment in the infrastructure of your premises or establishment (from electricity, water, and other services, to decoration, lighting and other considerations)

3. You must make expensive wholesale contracts with suppliers and suppliers and make an initial investment in the inventory or products with which you will start your real business.

4. You must invest in online and offline advertising (ranging from advertising just outside your Store, to traditional print advertising and some other online methods, such as Facebook, Instagram, and others.)

5. Expensive and bureaucratic local licenses and permits, Licenses, and other legal procedures that, on many occasions, are so expensive and time-consuming, that for some, they are an insurmountable obstacle.

6. Maintenance costs and services (utilities). You must pay for all the services associated with your establishment (electricity, water, gas, land use, property rent, employees, etc...)

7. You must continuously re-invest in new products by increasing your risks of store inventory that is not sold.

8. You have a minimal reach, not being able to sell much outside your community.

9. Among others...

So knowing how to do Dropshipping correctly helps you overcome many of these obstacles. Dropshipping vs. A traditional Store, as we have seen, has the following considerations in favor:

With Dropshipping:

1. You can sell to everyone, regardless of your location, because you sell online on your web domain.

2. The investment in creating your Online Store, with

all the technical and visual details required, is almost 75% less than the investment you would have made to create a physical establishment.

3. There are no expensive wholesale contracts or need to store inventory. Nor is a minimum purchase necessary to know how to do Dropshipping.

4. Investment in advertising is much more focused, usually with better returns on investment and in much less time. This is because you have access to the leading online advertising channels much more immediately (Facebook Ads, Google Adwords, YouTube, and Instagram Ads, Influencer Marketing, etc.)

5. Licenses, Permits, and other legal aspects (obviously with their variations in each country) are usually much more accessible, less expensive, and faster to obtain. In many countries there is a significant lack of regulation for online business, mainly in Latin America, so starting in a Dropshipping business, sometimes it also means explaining to your government what the model is and How to Do Dropshipping, so they can tell what the best way to fulfill your legal obligations is.

The best thing always is that you consult with someone who is an expert in legal aspects for online businesses, within your country. Commercial or commercial lawyers are usually the right place to start.

1. The maintenance costs are usually much lower, being reduced to a simple annual income of Domains, Lodgings, or a monthly income of some systems or applications that are used in your Online Store.

2. You do not need to "reinvest" in inventory. Although here I am referring to financial re-investment, if you must "reinvest" much of your time and effort in maintaining a fresh, updated and trending inventory for your Online Store, it does not mean that you need to buy the products beforehand, but to update your catalog directly in your Online Store, with new products from your Suppliers or suppliers.

3. Your reach can be worldwide, local, or as you decide. The limit is up to you.

4. Among others…

4. If you fail, losses are usually very acceptable, even welcome.

We are all afraid of failing, but above all, we are so scared of losing our money. With the Dropshipping model, the most significant loss you can suffer is in time and effort, since the investments you will have made in the infrastructure or technical and visual details of Your Online Store, usually recover shortly. And if for some reason you do not improve them, it is because perhaps you did not know how to do Dropshipping effectively or you gave up early.

Woo! What do you think about these advantages of Dropshipping so far? Can you think of any other?

Like any offline business, online businesses have risks, investment, and have disadvantages. To know how to do Dropshipping, it is necessary to understand the problems of the model and its potential setbacks.

Disadvantages of Dropshipping

1. You don't know the products you sell in detail.

This is because you usually do not have the products physically, but your supplier stores and sends them for you. This makes customer service difficult, so that the questions of your customers, often end up with you asking your supplier about this or that characteristic of the products, to answer your customer. This also means that customer service can be slower on your part, having to "triangulate" information with your provider for answers.

How to solve this? - Buy the products yourself, even if only one piece, to know them in detail physically.

2. Shipping Times are usually longer.

This is because many of your suppliers are on the other side of the world, and getting the products to your customer can take a long time. Customers usually look for fast shipping, and it can be a bit difficult to find the balance between the right supplier, the right product, the right price, and the correct shipping time.

How to solve this? - Negotiate with your suppliers to expedite your shipments, in exchange for increasing your marketing efforts, and you can also search for "local" or closer suppliers to your customers and offer much faster delivery. For example, if your target market is primarily in the United States, you can search for suppliers in the United States that offer better shipping times for your customers. This is usually the best option to expedite shipping times. That is, "bring your store closer to your customers."

3. Some Market Niches are highly saturated.

When I talk with my students of the Dropshipping Course, many of them intend to create their Online Stores with Dropshipping, in the same old niches.

Many of them do not know that there are specific Market Niches in Dropshipping that are incredibly saturated, unprofitable, and, frankly, a waste of time, money, and effort. Let's say, and it's a very common beginner's mistake. Let's learn a little now about Saturated Market Niches for Dropshipping.

Electronics. This is undoubtedly the worst Market Niche for Dropshipping. If you want to know how to do Dropshipping like a pro, stay away from electronics at all costs.

Electronics is a Dropshipping Market Niche much demanded by beginners. Either because it is to their liking, or because they feel that the products can be exciting for the buyers or that they can be profitable for themselves, but the reality is very distant from this. In the electronics market niche, we have the following:

- Cell phones, Smartphones, Tablets

- Cell Phone Accessories, Tablets

- Cases for Cell phones, Cases, Smart Cases, etc...

- Laptops and PCs

- Chargers for Cell phones, Power Banks, Replacement batteries for smartphones, etc...

- Electronic Cigars

- Televisions, Screens, Monitors, etc.

- Hearing aids, speakers, etc...

- Drones

All this is known as "Consumer Electronics" and is undoubtedly a collection of trendy products. But why is Electronics the worst Dropshipping Market Niche?

Well, there is a list of reasons (I hope convincing enough to get away from it):

1. The main places of purchase for this niche are eBay, Amazon, Mercado Libre, Linio, Wish, and the like.

2. On eBay and Amazon, 90% of the world's electronics providers are concentrated, which they sell directly to consumers (all major brands are selling on these sites directly to the final consumer, without intermediaries). This includes brands such as Apple, Samsung, Huawei, Microsoft, LG, Motorola, Intel, Bose, AMD, etc ...).

3. It is difficult to compete with the most popular vendors of these platforms. Consumer electronics sellers are usually sellers who have been selling on eBay, Amazon, etc. for many years... And today they offer excellent products, from well-known brands, in "bundles" or packages, with reasonable shipping times, good Discounts, even gifts. They have achieved these prices based on negotiations with the leading suppliers and because they went from "Dropshipping" to "Light Bulk," which is the wholesale medium. Many of these suppliers and vendors have agreements that offer even more significant discounts when they buy a specific volume of inventory.

4. Prices are shallow, margins almost non-existent.

This is a bit of the same. At Wish.com, you will find consumer electronics products from China, at ridiculous prices.

For example:

This "SmartWatch" type watch only costs USD 12. A price will be tough to beat. Firstly, because the product is undoubtedly coming from a Chinese supplier that offers the product directly from the factory without an intermediary. The second because if the customer pays 12$, it means that it costs less for the supplier to manufacture it. That is, to maintain its profitability and usefulness, they bet on a large volume of sales and do not give discounts to intermediaries in addition to the quality of the product, it will be well below the average.

What does this mean for you? Well, if you wanted to sell the same watch, first, you must get a supplier for this, second, the provider must offer the watch to you for less than USD 12 so that you can provide it in your minimum Online Store at the same price. And it also means that your profit margin can be tiny, and for it to be profitable for you, you should invest more in advertising to bet on volume sales, which can further diminish your profit if you target the wrong audience (let's say with Facebook Ads).

What are the chances of finding all this in your favor?

According to studies on electronic commerce, competing for the price on eBay, Amazon, Wish, etc... in Consumer Electronics has been the leading cause of abandonment and closure of up to 156,874 Online Stores opened between 2015 and 2018 in the first three months of operation.

The reasons simply approach profitability, lack of sustainability since when existing sellers face a new competitor (ie, TU), they merely lower prices a bit more (taking advantage of that luxury can be given) and they make you out of the market in a matter of days because they know you can't lower the price more than they do. So if you want to know how to do Dropshipping correctly and not go through this nightmare, please stay away from consumer electronics.

It is for your sake (and that of your wallet).

There are many other reasons to avoid the Consumer Electronics Niche, but I hope with this you understand the idea. Let's talk about different wrong market niches to start with Dropshipping:

1. Products of Brand or License or Trademark, etc... (because you are going to get into problems and lawsuits for offending property rights and trademarks)

2. Brand clothing or tennis (for that of Trademarks, resale licenses, etc...). This includes all sportswear, sports equipment, etc...

3. Toys of known brands "pirates" (for example, that the action figure resembles a known character, but is not original, or does not have the corresponding permits)

4. Firearms, Collection Swords, or similar (it is tough to overcome the customs problem for these products, in addition to that in many countries they are prohibited)

5. Health Products (because you can't risk that the product does not have the right process, the right ingredients, or the proper scientific support and can cause health problems for your customers, or even death. Believe me, and you don't want to risk the physical integrity of your clients or their health). This also includes all kinds of creams, supplements, pastes, beauty chemicals, etc...

6. Products for children or babies (for the same reasons as above)

7. Pirate products, not original, of low quality or replicas of innovative products

8. Movies, Videogames, and Music (unless you have a resale license)

Knowing how to do Dropshipping involves many things, and as you can see, it is a complicated business, although with many more advantages than disadvantages.

So... How to do Dropshipping and succeed in the shortest possible time?

In order not to be one more of the bunch that tries to put

up a Dropshipping business and fails or leaves soon, you must follow a proven, systematic structure that will help you have a much better chance of success.

There are many options for doing simple business from home, so you can also explore other options if you think Dropshipping is not for you. If you feel you are in the right place, then read on.

Start with an Audience and a Problem, before thinking about a Product.

When you think about your target market and how it hurts, what problems or obstacles you face, you take possession of a need and force you to feel like your potential customer. Knowing how to do Dropshipping implies that you can think like your client, understand your problem to offer a solution through your products.

Many believe that it is better to start with the product and then see who you sell it to, but in reality this only takes you away from making a real connection with your potential audience. And it takes away your abilities to enhance your brand, by not focusing from the beginning in solving a specific problem of your ideal group of clients.

To know how to do Dropshipping correctly, start with the audience, then with the product. Do not want to find the best jacket for snow and later try to sell it in the Caribbean. Better find a community of people who suffer from a lot of colds that are difficult to access good snow jackets and approach them with a solution.

Everything is based on the law of the success of Dropshipping: "Offer the right product to the right audience." So you know, How to do Dropshipping depends a lot on how you match your target market and your products.

∅ Invest time in choosing your business model and your sales platform

Here I mean that to know Dropshipping and how it works, it is not necessary to hurry. Take your time researching all the eCommerce platforms or Platforms for Online Stores that are available and take your time to choose the one that suits you best. You can investigate options like Shopify, Woocommerce, Prestashop, Wix, Magento (now part of Adobe), and many others.

∅ Invest in professional design

If you want to be professional, your Graphic Design should be too. So if you know Graphic Design for Online Stores, apply all your knowledge in the professional design of Your Online Store. If you do not have so many skills, you must invest in a Professional Design, quality, above average. If you want to know how to do Dropshipping correctly, invest in your design.

∅ Take your time in selecting your Audience and Market Niches

This will undoubtedly be crucial to your success, so it

should be what you spend the most time with. Analyze multiple types of audiences, their needs, tastes, hobbies, locations, income levels, problems and obstacles, purchasing power, etc...

This data will help you distinguish sales opportunities and be able to find and match the right product with the right audience.

∅ *Reinvest your earnings in marketing*

You must reinvest all your money (at least at the beginning) so that you make better marketing campaigns, better web content. And also that you invest in improving the speed, design, and functionality of your page and Online Store.

∅ *Create content marketing strategies*

Content remains the king, so take advantage of the capabilities and benefits of having a blog and talking about topics that may be of interest to your target audience. Talk about how to solve small problems that your audience suffers and try to match these with some of your products.

∅ Use paid to advertise as a sales strategy

Many times How to do Dropshipping means going beyond organic traffic and moving to paid traffic. This means that you must learn about Facebook Ads, Google AdWords, YouTube and Instagram Ads, and other channels that offer to approach your audience, in exchange for paid advertising campaigns.

Ø Don't forget the parties

Always have on hand a calendar of festivities, in which you can easily incorporate Coupons, Promotions, Special Events, Discounts, free shipping, and other tactics, to increase your orders during all the festivities (Christmas, New Year, Black Friday (Good End) in Spanish), Cyber Monday, Etc...)

Ø Always look for new products, new suppliers

Never forget to renew your catalog continually, never stop looking for new suppliers and look for better discounts, better negotiations, and always have a fresh, current and modern record, according to the needs of your audience. If you don't know where to get Dropshipping providers, try SaleHoo (the best provider directory currently available).

Ø Save a percentage of your income

Many entrepreneurs fail to start an Online Store with Dropshipping by not having savings for eventualities. Every business has unforeseen risks, risks, and unexpected difficulties. You must have savings to face unexpected situations that you did not have. If you want to know how to do Dropshipping efficiently, you must save for contingencies.

Ø **Take it seriously**

I'm tired of hearing the same story. «I didn't succeed with my Online Store,» «All that I already knew but I have not sold anything,» «You have not taught me anything new,» etc.… I had the opportunity to interview many of my students of the Dropshipping Course When I ask things like:

- How much time do you dedicate to your business?

- How much money do you invest in your paid advertising?

- How many Market Niches have you researched to date?

- How many products have you tried in Facebook campaigns?

- What are your current investment returns and your cost per click of your Facebook Ads campaigns (or any other PPC channel)?

- How many visits do you receive daily in Your Online Store?

- How do you bring traffic to your Online Store?

- When did your business start and how long have you been in it?

- What has been your content strategy?

- How do you measure your success, what metrics or KPI do you analyze every day?

- How do you handle your business finances? Do you have a statement of income, an accounting process, profit and loss sheet, etc ...?

- How much savings do you have for unforeseen business?

And similar questions, many people do not have these answers; they only dedicate little time; they don't invest in advertising. They have tried a few products (sometimes only a miserable Facebook campaign) and other similar answers. And the funny thing is that they are still surprised to have failed in the "attempt."

If you want to know how to do Dropshipping, you must have a mentality in which you see this as a serious, formal business and treat it as such. I doubt you have the success you are looking for if you only see it as a passing business or out of curiosity (unless it is merely that and does not expect great results).

∅ You must have a mindset of abundance and problem solving

The one who succeeds in Dropshipping, is an expert in solving problems, knows that every conflict has a solution, and does not "close the world" in How to Do Dropshipping, but seeks and finds solutions to all problems, or knows when to ask for help.

It is also essential that you have an abundance mentality, not an instant gratification mentality that seeks to obtain a miracle or millionaire profits within a few days. Having a new Online Store is the same as putting a new Restaurant in your community. It takes time to succeed, and there is a lot against you from the start that you will have to solve day by day.

And much more.

So in summary, let's list the recommendations in this chapter, so you know how to do Dropshipping and succeed in the shortest possible time:

1. Start with a hearing and a problem before thinking about a product.

2. Invest time in choosing your business model and your sales platform.

3. Invest in professional design

4. Take your time in selecting your Audience and Market Niches

5. Reinvest your earnings in marketing

6. Create content marketing strategies

7. Use paid to advertise as a sales strategy

8. Don't forget the parties.

9. Always look for new products, new suppliers

10. Save a percentage of your income

11. Take it seriously

12. You must have a mindset of abundance and problem solving

13. Measure everything and optimize it.

There you have it, knowing how to do Dropshipping is very important, especially if it is your first time in this type of business. So consider these recommendations when starting.

CHAPTER 5

AMAZON FBA

Nowadays, it is easier to sell on the internet thanks to online sales sites like Amazon. All types of products can be sold on the Web. But to be able to profit from it, it is necessary to be well informed on the operation of the site in question, to sell in all peace of mind. We must also choose the most popular sites so that a maximum sees the product of potential customers. We will see in this chapter how to make money on Amazon FBA.

Amazon FBA, how does it work?

Amazon FBA is an online sales site, offering its services as an intermediary between sellers and customers. Even an individual like me can benefit from Amazon FBA services to sell my products. In return, Amazon requires me a percentage according to the sale made. In spite of a rather high commission, Amazon is one of the most influential sites, which makes it possible to sell more quickly.

To make it easier for vendors, Amazon FBA is responsible for storing and delivering products ordered by customers. To do this, Amazon has several logistics centers spread throughout France and several European countries. To sell on Amazon, you must create a legal entity and have a professional account to be eligible on the sales platform, as a seller. Then, label the products to be sold and send them to the nearest logistics centers. The products in question will be available within 24 to 48 hours on the market.

Amazon is operational all over France, but also in Europe. It is possible to sell its products in Germany, Italy, the United Kingdom or Spain. Thanks to the European Pan service, Amazon allows you to operate locally or abroad, and your products will be delivered in less than 48 hours.

Register on Amazon

By accessing the Amazon site, information about you will be requested, such as:

- The credit card

- The details of the company

- The person receiving the service

Banking information

Opening an account on Amazon

The only admission criteria on Amazon is to have a professional account. By having this account, you will be able to benefit from the services of Amazon, in particular, the service "shipped by Amazon." Depending on your activity, you have a choice between two types of accounts:

- The Basic account

- The PRO account

1- The Basic account

Depending on the products, sellers make less than 40 sales monthly. This particularly concerns individuals. With this type of account, Amazon earns 0.99 euros per purchase.

2- The pro account

This type of account is ideal for professionals who offer a wide variety of products on the site. I think it's more reasonable because the platform requires a total of 30 euros per month for the subscription on the PRO account. But it is to know that the service "shipped by Amazon" is only accessible to those with a professional account. Once this account is in your possession, you will be able to access the platform. It will be enough for you to follow the indications to proceed to the sending of your product.

Fees and commissions on Amazon

Amazon is primarily a sales platform that connects sellers and customers. In return, the site requires receives a commission according to the sale made by each seller. There are two types of commissions on Amazon:

- Commissions based on the selling price

- Amazon FBA charges or "shipped by Amazon."

Commissions based on the selling price

This type of commission concerns the fees required by Amazon according to the sales made. The price varies according to the kind of product. Indeed, every type of product is categorized, and each category has a commission grid.

Amazon FBA fees

This type of charge is for the "shipped by Amazon" service. Which means to charge against another commission, the management of the products of each seller. The site deals with storage, sale, product preparation, and delivery. From now on, it is this type of efficient service that has made Amazon the world leader in E-commerce. The order processing fee varies depending on the weight of the product. For example, the processing fee for a product of 250 g is 2.55 euros.

Pros and cons with Amazon FBA

- Advantages

Selling on Amazon provides several benefits, not only for the seller but also for the buyer.

- ### Efficiency and time savings

Selling a product has become an easy task on Amazon. No need to move, or look for customers, without success all day. Just send the product to the nearest Amazon logistics center, and you're done.

The service "shipped by Amazon" is also the highlight of the site. It allows sellers of other income-generating activities while Amazon is responsible for selling the product and delivering it to the buyer. If this task was the responsibility of a professional seller, it should surely proceed to recruitment, which would considerably increase its expenses, and reduce its gains. With this type of Amazon service, the seller is a winner.

- **Reliable and fast service**

Amazon uses effective means to sell its products. Buyers can subscribe to Amazon premium for a fee of 49 euros per year. In this way, they will have access to videos presenting several categories of products available on the platform. Also, 30 free trial days are offered on Amazon Prime. Thus, the products you put on sale will be much more likely to be identified by potential customers.

- **Customer satisfaction**

Unlike vendors who do not use the "shipped by Amazon" service, those who benefit from it can gain the trust of customers through the speed of delivery. As a result, the seller has no risk of having his account suspended because he will avoid any worries with the buyers. Indeed, the reason for the suspension of an account often a problem of sale, as an unsatisfied customer who cancels his purchase. But this is, in most cases, the sellers who take care of the delivery themselves, and who do not respect the conditions of sale of Amazon.

- The inconvenient

- ***Risk of dependence on Amazon***

Selling on Amazon exposes the seller to a risk of dependency. Indeed, once used to use this platform, it is possible that the seller does not think about doing other activities. However, a product may be challenging to sell.

- **Closure of account**

A level of performance is required on Amazon. This requirement concerns the quality of the product and the ability of the seller to process the mails. If these requirements are not met, the vendor's account may be suspended. Fortunately, training is provided to those who need it to avoid this inconvenience. If you want to benefit, I advise you to conduct research training on Amazon FBA. You'll find experienced and successful salespeople who share their experiences with choosing the right product, managing sourcing, integrating the product with Amazon, and anything that can help make Amazon profitable.

- **Profitability on Amazon**

At first glance, the commissions that Amazon requires seem to be considerable. But if we calculate the charges without using the Amazon FBA service, we will find that they are higher.

I think that taking care of delivery is even complicated. First, the product must be packaged in good shape before shipment. With several products to be delivered daily, it will be necessary to make recruitments.

There is a lot more chance of selling quickly on Amazon compared to other online sales sites because this platform is among the most used in the world.

- ***Choice of product to put on sale***

The choice of product to sell is critical because it will consider buying a number to get enough storage. You will face a considerable loss if the product is not sold once online.

- ***Avoid overly heavy products***

As we have seen later, the more the product is heavy, the more Amazon FBA fees are essential. Opt for a space-saving product.

- **Use effective software**

To be sure, the right product, I think it is necessary to use the software, to assess the most wanted products on Amazon quickly. This will give you access to relevant information, such as the estimated number of sales of a specific product, or the comments of buyers. The software then indicates through a note, whether the product is exciting or not. These tools are certainly paying, but they are worth the cost to make sure they are profitable.

Learn about the influence of the product on potential buyers

For a product to sell, it must be accessible. Several clues

help to identify a profitable product. A lot of comments mean that the product is of interest to a lot of people. You can also find out on the site by accessing the "best sellers" tab. In this way, you will see the most sold items, and you will be able to get inspired to find the products to put on sale.

Other useful information is issued on the platform. By informing you about the number of customers who have purchased a product, the platform makes available to you other items purchased by the same customers. You will then have a wide choice of products according to your budget.

However, it is necessary to check the seasonality of the chosen product, as it may only sell for a specified period.

Estimate of sale

Once the product is chosen, it will be necessary to fix a price before putting it on sale on Amazon.

- **Use positioning strategy**

You need to position yourself against competitors, mainly if you sell the same type of product. But it is not necessary to use this strategy if the product is high-end. Indeed, you can afford to sell a high price if your product is of high quality.

Online sales platforms make it easy to sell products.

Individual or professional, this site allows all types of sellers to sell quickly, using the influence of the platform from potential buyers. With the Amazon FBA service, the seller can confidently trust Amazon with the tasks of storing, preparing, and shipping the product. But to be profitable on this site, you must know how to choose the product in fashion, by inquiring on the site itself or by using various tools available on the Web.

CHAPTER 6

AFFILIATE MARKETING?

"Earn money online" is a trendy term among search engines and if you are creating quality content and don't have the level of influence to get your line of products/services or sell your book as well as influencers such as Aida Domenech, Yuya or Luisa FernandaW; Affiliate Marketing is for you.

What's affiliates marketing?

Affiliate marketing consists of promoting third-party products on your website. Although when talking about it, we may use the term "sell," we do not sell, but rather induce sales. The idea is that you exercise online sales and, when you get a deal for others, you take a commission.

Technically, the system is that simple:

- The visitor enters your website, and a link is found that leads to a product purchase page.
- This link has a personalized code that identifies you so that the store knows that it is a customer; you send it to you.
- If your visitor makes the purchase, you take a commission.

The above definition is generic, as each company with an affiliate program can put the clauses it deems appropriate. For example, some programs only support links on web pages, others that also support social networks or connections sent by e-mail, etc. Also, the duration of the cookie varies. That is the correct time from when the user first clicks on the link until he can make the purchase with a commission for you. It can be one day, 5, one month... whatever the store decides. Finally, each company offers the percentages it wants, either 5% or 20% commission, for example.

Necessary, do not take a penny for the visitor to see your recommendation or even click (this is not Adsense). It only gives money the purchase within the fixed term.

Thanks to it, you can generate passive income by monetizing your content, not only with a blog or a website but also with your social networks.

When deciding to use this method, as an affiliate, you will not have a minimum or maximum ceiling. That is, from any pile, you can start to generate income. Although some Affiliate Marketing platforms establish a value from which you can charge and the days on which you can perform this operation.

They are programs that pay you for conversions that are made through the links that you put on your website. In more precise words, you are paid a percentage for each sale or action that a user makes through a link hosted on your site.

By the way, obtaining passive income means establishing mechanisms to later earn money without spending more effort. Do not confuse with not dedicating any effort. To generate passive income, you always have to work well, and affiliate marketing is no exception. It is not «free money,» nor is it a bargain, distrust who sells you «motorcycles.»

What a way to take away the desire to read the chapter, right? Not at all, affiliate marketing is more than impressive (that's why I dedicate an entry to it), but the sales world is full, and it's not my role.

Do not doubt that affiliate marketing is one of the most stable ways to make money online, along with advertising (Adsense). But to achieve this, we have to find the right product for the right target, become a reference on that topic and position well.

You can also create your tracking link and do Affiliate Marketing. This works, when on your account you place advertising on your blog, for example, through a contract with a brand, giving the possibility to agree to your conditions.

The good news, as I indicated at the beginning, is that you can also implement it using your profiles on Youtube, Facebook, or Twitter. But be careful not Instagram, since this social network is very meticulous in that matter and prevents inserting links unless it is a sponsored post.

Large media in online presence use it. The Affiliate Marketing system works like this:

An X / У visitor enters your website, either through referral, direct, social media, organic traffic, etc. Upon arriving at your site, he observes a link in the form of a banner, for example, and he decides to click.

The link you host, you should try to be as natural as possible, as if it were part of the design of your page and what you recommend (be it product or service) be by the content. Now, continuing, when the visitor clicks, that link takes him to a purchase page of that product, causing that lead to entering the sales to funnel and even more of the purchase.

The link is personalized, and some platforms allow you to follow up. This is the way the store knows that that potential buyer sent it to you.

With Affiliate Marketing, you don't earn by click or impressions. You earn a commission that is usually very generous when the visitor finishes the purchase, and it is a bit similar in that regard to the discount codes that some influencers give their audience.

On YouTube, for example, some YouTube users use this platform to link advertising between their content. Generally, it has to do with the theme of your videos, or they are certain brands with an excellent reputation, with some launch, new product, or suggestion.

These characters earn for each click, action, and purchase that was made through those links. It is valid to note that they not only use Affiliate Marketing to insert links, it also has to do a bit with the Google and Adsense Display Network.

Now, this advertising that sometimes makes us annoying when we are watching a video on that social network and suddenly appears in the form of banners, in-stream, or other formats available on the same YouTube. The income you get depends on the type of action and your CPA (Cost per Action).

That is, it is not the same to earn money by registering on a particular website, buying a product at a discount, or downloading an application.

To give you part of the answer, let me tell you that it is possible to make money with Affiliate Marketing, the trick is to do it, and I recommend it.

As I said, it is possible, but you have to know-how, and the main thing is to which audience you are going to direct your efforts. Identify the appropriate target, which is similar to the content integrated with your website, that is to know how the system works because, in the future, you can experiment with varied topics, yes, try to have a particular relationship with your brand.

The right choice of the type of products/services you will take through Affiliate Marketing is crucial. You should look consistent and build credibility because there is no reason for you to talk about healthy eating, for example. And include links to video games or something like that, unless they have to do with the central issue, so it is indirect.

With the previous example, I want to show that consistency is nothing more than the key to "sell" and achieve a good conversion ratio.

Affiliate Marketing Classes

Let's get to the point!

There are different kinds of Affiliate Marketing. Then I will refer to the most prominent and so you can go checking which option is best for you according to your goals, and it costs nothing to try!

PPC Affiliates are those included in the search engine results, and it is the traffic that affiliates take advertisers to your website. It has to do with an SEM strategy, and keywords are used:

- **Websites and blogs:** with these sites, you generate content, which can be related to a product/service or be attractive to an advertiser. Generally, it's paid by commission, and they are usually very high because it is a direct recommendation, achieving a registration, affiliation, a purchase, etc.

- Cashback and sites are how the Amazon platform works at the level of Affiliate Marketing. What he does is share the income with the users. You can get commission either represented in money, discount, or redeemable points, every time a sale is consolidated through your link.

- **E-mail marketing databases:** if you become an affiliate with this system, you will know what I am talking about in this item. By having a website or blog, you will have a database with subscribers or people who left your data in exchange for a downloadable example. Well, this type of Affiliate Marketing allows you to transfer that data from registered users, segmented by interests related to the product/service.

- **Social media:** it is an alternative for an effective and real influencer because you have to have the capacity to impact, reach and impressions to do the job of generating quality lead for the advertiser that hires you.

- *Affiliation networks:* they are platforms that connect advertisers and affiliates. Some like TradeDoubler, ClickBank, Amazon, and its network of affiliates in Spanish and others, where you should check that they have credibility because there is a pair that is hunting for unsuspecting.

Affiliate Marketing Portals

Did you get here well let's continue! The proliferation and increase of internet sales strengthen this type of platform, which aims to be intermediaries between advertisers and affiliates, and the best is free.

These portals provide you with a code, at the time you register as an affiliate. With that same link code, you can track.

Advertisers who are registered are the ones who choose if they decide to work with you under this modality. I have chosen three that I find very interesting:

- *Afiliapub*

An affiliate network gathers online bets of many types, such as sports, online games, among others, and offers you different ways to monetize your space with very professional promotional tools.

Afiliapub is available in Spain and Latin America. In it, you can find and have access to different campaigns to monetize your website and blog.

Access to massive commissions ranging between $ 50 and $ 250 per lead and are paid via platforms such as bank transfer and PayPal (in Colombia, you can already get money with PayPal through Neque).

It also gives you $ 20 (dollars) of bonuses just for signing up. Pay $ 100 per CPA that is, each user registration and 25% per commission, of any activity registered by the referred user, thanks to you.

• *Shopify Affiliates*

Shopify, in this aspect, motivates its advertisers to create their affiliate program. If you still didn't know, Shopify is an eCommerce platform, where anyone, not only entrepreneurs, can open an online store.

It's like eBay and even the same Amazon that I will mention below, but among its differences in addition to the App and 24/7 support, it is the commission for sales it charges, which ranges from 2% in its necessary rate to 0.5% in the most expensive, the price that applies to advertisers.

• *Clickbank*

It is the favorite of many and has become popular among those who sell services, as it bets on the promotion of intangibles and product information. That is where you can find e-books, recipes, and more related.

With Clickbank, you can earn commissions of up to 75% of the total product/service sold on the platform.

Amazon, the grand bazaar of affiliation

Though we have, discuss it in the previous chapter, but to explain better what affiliating marketing is. It is worth stopping at Amazon because it has the most extensive affiliate program there is. This has significant advantages, for example:

Being a store in which everyone consumes brings confidence to the user. And it is that our reader may trust us, but if we send him to a store that does not sound like him, he may not dare to buy. With Amazon, this will never happen.

We have an extensive catalog. Amazon is sold almost everything, even things we do not know or exist, so we can look for niches not yet exploited or focus specifically on that product or range of products that define us most.

Finally, although we are going to focus on a niche, because it is more effective (think about it, you cannot be an expert at all) if the visitor enters Amazon with our link but ends up buying another different product, we will also take a commission. This is not going to happen with affiliate programs focused on a single product. But, the cookie only lasts 24 hours.

It is also essential to clarify what is surely Amazon's biggest hit. Although the operation is similar, the Amazon of each country has its own utterly independent affiliate system. In other words, if you want to sell products from Amazon.es, Amazon.com, and Amazon.co.uk (for example), you have to register in 3 different systems. This results in unfortunate situations such as that if you have a blog and sell with amazon.es affiliate system, a user, for example, from Colombia, will not generate commission even if you buy. There are plugins to solve these situations, but input is somewhat cumbersome.

This also generates certain legal loopholes in the sense that for example in the USA they are stricter and it is relatively easy to win a ban if you violate any of its rules (as usually happens with these things, many people start using it without having clear rules to 100%).

The Amazon panel is also very good with a product search engine that offers you the final link with your affiliate code, as well as banners.

Other affiliate networks

iTunes: The purchase of music by iTunes is increasingly popular in Spain, although its limitation will also make it challenging to find a niche.

eBay: A classic and enjoyable alternative to Amazon, for its international fame and reliability.

Aliexpress Portals: The affiliation service of the leading Chinese trade company is an exciting option. Its catalog is also vast, although it is true that there is still more reluctance to make significant money purchases. The same can be said of the even Chinese Gearbest.

Last but not least, we have the affiliate product agglutination, such as CJ Affiliate, Zanox, Shareasale, or

Clickbank. Although these websites do not sound like you, they are agencies that carry a lot of brands and products and act as intermediaries to sell their products through blogs like yours.

Essential Ways To Use Affiliate Marketing

Once we know the basic rules of affiliate marketing and if we want to use it, we have to see how it fits our project.

Affiliate Marketing in a Blog

If we have a blog in which we publish content regularly, we will be interested in detecting products that may interest our audience and talk about them. In this case, we should do more natural affiliate marketing, as if we recommend something to a friend, only by explaining things in more detail. We are interested in being honest and recommending good things because, although we want to generate sales, our reputation is more important.

For example, you have a gardening blog, and there is a type of fertilizer for geraniums that you have tried, and it is especially useful. If you are going to talk about it well in your blog, it is possible that thanks to you, that product takes some purchase. With affiliate marketing, you can take advantage of this.

It is also not necessary that you love the product. You can make a comparison of 5 types of subscriptions and do affiliate marketing with the 5. Surely you will recommend one (you will not be one of those who make comparatives and drop a roll not to make things clear, right?), but you can put purchase links at 5. If you say this is the worst, but your reader prefers to buy it for anything (maybe it is cheaper), it is not your problem.

For a blogger, this system is advantageous because you do not need to force the sale of the product, but to present your opinion (with data, where appropriate) and advise the purchase. To the reader, buying that product will cost the same, so if you buy it with the added value of the recommendation of someone who deserves reliability, then better for both. And for the product or store creator.

Niche or e-commerce affiliation page

If, on the other hand, you are interested in affiliate marketing so much that you want to go all out with it, you may want to make a website exclusively to sell products or even a web store of related products. The advantages of this type of project are apparent; you just set up the web and make optimized texts. Neither do you charge the customer, or send the product or offer after-sales service. Instead, you receive a percentage for each product you sell.

Although to set up such a project, you have first to find the right niche that is not exploited and with the potential to generate exciting income. You also have to develop a well-formed website in terms of SEO and UX to facilitate both organic searches and the buying process. He has his crumb. If you think it's just about entering Amazon, deciding that you're going to sell laptops and start earning pasta while scratching your belly, you're pretty wrong.

Without a doubt, affiliate marketing is one of the most stable ways to make money online, especially when we talk about generating relatively passive income. But the success of your affiliate marketing will only come by doing things right and not without a good dose of trial and error.

CHAPTER 7

REAL ESTATE

Real estate investments represent an exciting and profitable alternative for those who are looking to generate new sources of income.

Among the different ways to earn money today, real estate investments have gained a significant boom in recent times worldwide.

This is because real estate investments represent an attractive market to grow long-term equity. However, to succeed in this branch, it is essential to soak up everything related to this field and be continually learning.

For most people, entering the world of real estate investments can be a complicated task, mainly when they have sold us the idea that large sums of money are needed, and that only a few can invest in real estate.

However, regardless of whether you are a small investor or have the savings of your entire life, real estate investments are an option and a very profitable market in which you can put your money to work.

The first thing you should know about real estate investments:

Before explaining how you can make money with real estate investments, we have to tell what they consist of and what their definition is. Real estate investments are those non-movable assets, such as buildings and land, with which rental, sale, and purchase transactions can be made.

Investments in real estate are made for different purposes: to obtain medium and long term profits, to obtain income through a subsequent sale or, to obtain both.

In fact, in the face of the economic crises that the world economy has been presenting, real estate investments become a "safe investment," since this falls on necessities, which means that people will always need a roof to sleep on.

How To Start In The World Of Real Estate Investments?

To start making money with real estate, it is essential, although it seems obvious, to have a property.

You indeed need capital to start. However, there are alternatives if you have a smaller budget. That is, money, to some extent, is not an excuse for not starting in the world of real estate investments.

For example, a new modality could help you if you have fewer monetary resources. This is known as real estate crowdfunding, which consists of a method with which several people, contributing a certain amount of money, can buy a property.

With crowdfunding, you can invest in several real estate projects, and you can do it from different websites, such as Housers or Bricks & People.

Now, if you have enough capital to start on your own, the first thing you should do is choose what type of property you would like to invest in.

You can choose between homes, commercial premises, storage rooms, garages, urban land, or rustic plots, where each of the options has different demands and requirements since it is not the same to manage commercial premises than a land.

Below we explain how to generate income with the different real estate investments, which will depend on the type of asset and the duration of your investment.

Methods to invest in real estate:

- **Lease:**

Leasing is one of the most traditional ways to earn money with real estate investments. This consists of renting your property to obtain an income, which is usually received every month, although this may vary according to the terms set in the contract.

Some of the complications that can be generated with this

income method are the following:

Sometimes, the tenant can call you to resolve property maintenance issues. For example, it may be that a key has been damaged and you need to solve the problem. One solution may be to hire damage insurance or hire a maintenance company.

There is also a risk that the tenant will fall into default, which can be solved with default insurance and studying, before signing the contract, the solvency history of the tenant.

Additionally, for a better guarantee, you can ask a person to endorse the tenant, also sign the contract and be in solidarity with the commitment.

Another problem with which we can run into is the deterioration of the property. This happens in the long term and will require that you make investments, or save money, for such repairs in the future.

- *Sale of the property:*

Another way to get money from a property is to sell it. The resale of the furniture can occur in various circumstances.

- *Overtime:*

Usually, the properties typically increase in price over time, even if you do not make any changes. The Consumer Price Index increases, the cost of living goes up and, therefore, the goods increase their market value. In the long run, selling your property will give you profits thanks to the valuation of your property.

- ### *Reform and sell later:*

If you have done some works to improve the property, you can sell in a matter of months and make a lot of profits. If you received the property in adverse conditions, you can make the corresponding arrangements and put them on sale. It will always be worth much more than when you bought it.

This type of business requires that you see the potential of the product, that is, although the current situation of the property is not the best, other aspects such as the location, the projection of the area, neighbors and future projects, make this property an attractive real estate investment.

- ### *Sell with criteria:*

What many would call luck in business, real estate investment experts know as criteria? Some properties are below the price due to different factors.

There are property owners that require liquidity, either for other businesses, needs, or commitments, which makes them willing to sell said property for a lower price.

This type of case demonstrates the importance of liquidity in the world of real estate investments. It is essential to have available capital to take advantage of this type of business opportunity that will generate very interesting profits in the short term.

In conclusion, you can buy cheap you can resell this property for a higher price in a matter of days or months.

Advantages of real estate investments:

If you are considering the possibility of starting to make real estate investments, in this section, we will explain what the benefits offered by real estate are.

You don't have to be an expert:

To make money on real estate investments, you don't have to be an economics specialist or have a degree in finance or law. To start, you have to know some basic concepts, and as you go forward, you will learn more.

It is better than saving:

Savings interest rates are meager in banks, which does not guarantee a substantial increase in your money. If you decide to invest that money in a property, your capital will increase, since these tangible assets are not affected by economic variables.

The properties increase their value by their location and the plans that exist for that area.

You can get extra income:

Real estate allows you to obtain medium and long-term profits due to the possibility of renting them. In many countries, people seek to lease a home due to the difficulties that exist when accessing a mortgage loan and due to rising housing prices.

If you need it, you can use it:

Having a home - or any other real estate - can benefit you in several economic, but also personal aspects. When you own a property, you can dispose of it in case of any emergency.

Advantage against inflation:

Real estate properties also have power over inflation. In the long term, the property will be revalued, and its price will be above the inflationary percentage. An example: we buy a home when prices have been high, but after a few years, it is likely to be worth more.

Opportunities to make a profit on real estate investments will always be present. Profitability in this field is assured if things are done correctly and care is taken.

How to avoid being scammed and other existing risks in real estate investment:

As in any other business, regardless of whether they are real estate investments, starting a business, or investing in gold, some unscrupulous people seek to affect investors.

It is no secret that you should be very careful when closing agreements or contracts to avoid being scammed. In these real estate businesses, having an expert lawyer on the subject turns out to be a great advantage.

Here are a series of recommendations that will prevent you from falling into traps and putting your equity or investment capital at risk, and more when you begin to discover the world of real estate investments.

Buy a property that is occupied:

By investing in real estate, you have significant capital to take care of. So before closing the purchase of a property, study the titles of the property and perform a preliminary inspection on-site to make sure that third parties do not occupy the property.

Failure to do this diligence can lead you to go through a long period of courts to remove the occupants, resolving a conflict of interest and ultimately losing a return on your capital.

Beware of fake money:

This may sound a bit silly, but there is a real risk of being paid with counterfeit money when you sell or rent your own. If you are a foreign investor and do not know the local currency by heart, it can happen to you.

How can you prevent this from happening? It is essential that you can familiarize yourself with the legal monetary environment of the country in which you reside - and of your own - or rely on a trusted person who can help you in this regard. Avoid being homeless and without money.

Another risk is that you receive checks without funds or promises of money transfers after making the transfer of the property. The best thing you can do for your peace of mind is that, until you see the money in your account, do not sign any contract.

Attention to contracts:

If you trust a real estate agency to manage the rental or sale of your property, be very careful with the agents that work with your property.

For example, the agent can write a contract of sale in which his commission is quite high. Also, you can place a clause stating that he will earn the commission even if the purchase has not been made.

This risk is related to the fine print of contracts in real estate investments, so read very well and have a trusted lawyer to review the contracts for you.

Other ways to lose your money by scams:

Besides, when it comes to acquiring a good, you can lose all the money through different scam methods:

A flat house that is not built: This can happen because the construction work is not finished by bankruptcy does not have the guarantee or insurance that guarantees the amounts contributed, and the land is not free of charges, the property belongs to a third party or You bought a good that is not being built.

When you buy an already built property: There may be unreported charges, the existence of several owners, and one of them refuses to sell, mortgages, debts, etc.

As we have already said, real estate investments are quite delicate due to the high sum of money that moves in them, but this does not have to be an excuse to avoid making money in this field.

There is a way to avoid these inconveniences and thus have a satisfactory experience in real estate investments. A practical and safe method of preventing a scam is by going to the Land Registry offices. There we can confirm that a property exists and the real owners of the property in question.

On the other hand, if we want to enter the world of real estate crowdfunding, we also have to pay close attention to the conditions imposed by the platform with which we are going to work.

It is essential to take care of ourselves in all aspects. Think about how money works and the best way to protect it.

Conclusions of real estate investments:

The final advice and one of the most important when it comes to investing in real estate are to be very cautious when making an investment decision.

Be sure to inform yourself about the conditions and characteristics of the properties, as well as do not forget to consult with experts in the field to guide you during the process.

Investing in a good is a great idea, especially if you want to secure your economic future and that of your family. The numbers speak for themselves worldwide.

Keep this in mind: there will always be someone who needs a roof to live in, a place to locate your business, or a garage to store your car. Be creative! The opportunities and money are there; with an excellent real estate investment, you can get them.

CHAPTER 8

HOW TO MAKE MONEY WITH A PODCAST

Although podcasts promise to "eat" on the radio until now, there was no direct way to earn money with podcasts. In this chapter, we will see all the options we have to monetize podcasts and the most profitable platforms to make podcasting your profession.

But let's start with the basics:

What is a podcast?

By definition, a podcast is a digital audio publication (video as well) that can be downloaded from the internet or listened to online. Put, it is like a radio program, but customizable. The name comes from "iPod" and "Broadcast," because before, they were only heard on iPods through iTunes. Nowadays, you can listen to it on countless platforms, websites, blogs, etc...

What is the most crucial factor in making money with a podcast?

As with most content on the Internet, like a blog or the YouTube platform itself, when it comes to generating money, the essential thing in the first place are the visualizations (visits) and subscribers. No matter how good your content is, if nobody listens to it, you don't earn money. This is logical. Of course, to have subscribers, the content must be excellent and exciting.

Create a Podcast

This is a strategy to make money online very interesting, which not only can generate a lot of income, but also can change your life and become a famous and influential person.

But let's go slowly. First, we answer the following question:

People can download podcasts and listen to them whenever they want.

The particularity of podcasts is that people can subscribe to them through an RSS feed.

The good thing about podcasts is that they personalize the interaction with our audience much more since our voice is much more powerful than the lyrics on a screen.

Throughout this chapter, we will cover all aspects so that you learn to make a successful podcast and use it for your online business, which is the objective of this section.

How to create a successful Podcast?

To create a Podcast and earn money online, you must carefully read and understand the following instruction:

1. Define the Objective and choose the Theme of a Podcast

What is the purpose of your Podcast?

Podcasts can become potent marketing tools.

Some of the world's most famous bloggers make monthly podcasts and ensure that half of the traffic on their sites comes from podcasts.

For many other professionals, the creation of a podcast has given them visibility, visibility, and prestige. Therefore, when making a podcast, it is essential to define the objective, because if you want to make a successful podcast, you must dedicate the effort it deserves.

Among the most common objectives are:

- Obtain prestige and visibility

- As a Marketing tool to sell affiliate products and send traffic to a website

- Expand an idea or cause

- Entertain or have fun

- Create content to retain our audience

The goal may change, there are many cases of people who have started podcasts to have fun and then have realized that they can make a tremendous economic profit from it and transform it into a big business.

There are also cases of people who have started podcasts for some reason (for example, environment) and have become real celebrities, with hundreds of thousands of followers.

What is essential to understand is that although the objective can change, it is important to define it at the outset because the whole strategy is going to be tied to that objective.

Choose the theme of your podcast

As an online entrepreneur, one can (and should) have a broad portfolio of ventures, blogs, online stores, forums, niche sites, etc.

With a podcast, it is different, in the vast majority of cases people will not create more than one podcast, and the reason is that you are exposed a lot and it is not convenient to position yourself as an expert or specialist in several things, one must point to your niche with all.

That is why choosing the theme of your podcast well is essential, it must be something that you are passionate about and that I redeemed, because success comes after a while, and for this, you will have dedicated many hours of life in your life.

No one says that you will not be able to change your mind and start over in two years, but then you will have wasted valuable time.

So, take time to choose the right topic, brainstorm the topics that you are most passionate about, and those that you think people would like to hear at home or on public transport.

The themes of your podcast can be as varied as niches exist, for example:

- Health tips
- Business and investments
- Politics
- Marketing
- Capital market
- Meditation
- Radio show
- Humorous program
- Recommendations on how to lead a healthy life
- Family and children
- Tips for pregnant women
- Sports and recreation
- A program about your favorite sports team
- Religion and spirituality
- Movie Theater
- Technology
- Games
- Hobbies

The list goes on, the best way to know if there is a community for your podcast is to do a small search on Google and see how many web pages and forums exist on the subject, the better, it means that there is a relevant audience.

Once you define the goal and theme, you can move on to the next step in creating your successful podcast.

2. The technology needed to make a successful Podcast

To create a good podcast, you will need to acquire some appropriate technology so that the quality of your recording is excellent. Nothing worse than an audio file that sounds bad. If you want to create a successful podcast, you must make it look professional, for this, you must acquire at least one good microphone. Below you will find some options at affordable prices so you can launch your podcast as soon as possible. At the end of the chapter, you will also find some essential programs to record and edit your podcast. The free options are equally good and recommended that you pay, so don't pay for something you don't need.

Microphones

- Heil PR-40 (XLR connection - not USB) Audio-Technica ATR2100 (USB and XLR connection) Samson C01UCW (USB connection) Blue Snowflake (USB connection)

Headset

- Plantronics Audio 995 Wireless

Podcast Kits

- Behringer C-1 Microphone with USB Mixer & Accessories

Software

- Software to record calls made by Skype (Mac)

- Pamela. Skype Call Recorder (PC and Mac)

3. Planning and preparing the content of a podcast

A prevalent mistake made by many people who start a podcast is to take the microphone and start talking. In 1% of cases, it is possible that the person has a natural talent and can make the recording excellent, but for the rest of us, mortals things require a little more time and preparation.

To prepare a podcast, you have two main options:

The first is to script it completely. Professional and successful podcasts are usually scripted. The person who creates the podcast (or in some cases hired auxiliary people) works on a script that will cover the full development of the podcast from beginning to end.

Writing a podcast allows for no empty moments, or to use molehills or take too many turns to explain an idea.

Scripted podcasts are a pleasure for the audience because

the announcer goes to the point of the topics he speaks and seems much more reliable and more robust.

The second option is to prepare a general structure with the different topics and then improvise on each theme. Most people who have podcasts choose this option because the time of dedication is much shorter.

In this case, the person defines four or five main themes and then develops them as if he were talking with a friend or telling something to a work colleague. This type of option is in favor of the spontaneity of the announcer, but this option is against the fact that there will be moments of doubt, moments of silence, possible use of a crutch and moments when too much is tried to explain an idea or the wrong words are used.

- **Interviews**

Interviews are very common among those who have podcasts. In the case of conducting an interview, all the questions that the respondent wants to ask himself should be written in advance (although you may not end up using them), calculating that extra time will have to be left for the interviewee to propose his topics and we must also consider improvising on the progress.

The best interviews are not structured too much, and the idea is that the person flows and is a constructive dialogue. The questions serve as support so that every time you feel that a topic has run out, there is a new trigger.

What should not be done?

Do not plan, take a microphone, and start talking. That, in addition to being very unprofessional, will end up frustrating our followers, because everything that has not been planned in most cases ends up being of poor quality.

Planning a podcast correctly also means managing the times. Be clear about how long it will take us to write the script, how long it will take us to record it, how long to edit it, and how much to upload and publicize it.

If your podcast has a specific frequency, you must be clear about the times, although you will find out with practice.

What content to create for a podcast?

Those who decide to listen to your podcast will do so because your content is excellent. Take the time to identify the topics that may interest your audience the most, and offer them value.

4. Create the identity and voice of a podcast

Before creating your podcast, you must decide about the character you want to give it. By this, I mean that you must previously imagine what kind of energy you want to transmit to your audience.

The identity of a podcast covers many things. Next, we will analyze some of the most important:

- **The rhythm of the voice**

Will you use an accelerated (excited) rhythm? Will you use a calm and leisurely rhythm? If you have a podcast about meditation and yoga, you probably choose a quiet rhythm, but if you have a podcast about fashion and celebrities, you are likely to pick a faster pace.

- **Tone**

The tone of your voice is also a matter that makes the podcast's identity. Always avoid being monotonous, add emotion to your words by raising and lowering the tones of your voice. If you speak all the time in the same tone of voice, you will bore the audience.

- **Humor**

The use of fun is a powerful weapon, but it can also be a double-edged sword. It is unfortunate when someone tries to be funny, and does not come out, generates rejection in the audience.

If you think you can and you know how to use humor, do it, but it is preferable not to do so.

It is also important not to abuse humor unless your podcast is humorous.

- **Emotion**

This is a fundamental point. When you do your podcast, you must convey emotion to your followers. They should feel that it is you talking to them and that the topics you develop passionate you.

Even if you choose severe themes and a calm and leisurely rhythm, you can convey the necessary emotion.

- **Interaction**

Mobilizing followers is something we must do all the time. This is done by asking questions or assumptions. For example, if we are talking about online business, we can ask, "... does it happen to them that they spend a lot of time looking at statistics instead of writing articles? If so, then the best thing is... "This is what the person on the other side immediately identifies with our speech, and they will surely be thinking"... yes yes, it happens to me all the time, what do I do?"

Now suppose your podcast is about relationships, then they make the following assumption "... Likely, they have ever broken your heart; in those cases, it is essential..." And the person on the other side will think "... well yes, they've broken my heart What should I do in those cases?"

Try to make your podcast a conversation with an imaginary audience, since you don't have anyone to answer you, and you must include the question in the story and answer it.

- **Speech**

What words will you use? Will you speak with famous words? Will you use a technical language?

It is always preferable to be as brief as possible and to the point. Do not fill your podcast with unnecessary information or take too long to get to the point.

What you say is the most important thing, and the content is the reason why your followers will listen to your podcast, make sure it is excellent.

- **Dynamic**

Your podcast should be entertaining, even if it is a severe podcast. A fascinating podcast is a progressive podcast. If possible, mix sounds, music, and other voices to enrich the audience's experience.

5. Tips to Record a Podcast Successfully

Once we have completed the previous steps of this tutorial, and we already have the necessary technology and the content of our podcast, we will go to record it.

Tips for recording the podcast

As you create podcasts, it will be more natural and more automatic, like any skill you learn from practice. But to reduce the chances of error, I will give you some essential tips to keep in mind when recording the podcast:

1- If more than one person participates in the podcast, they should never speak at the same time, doing so results in unintelligible sounds or "noise" for our audience.

2- Take breaks every so often that gives a respite to the listener and gives him time to assimilate what you say.

3- Use a soundtrack, but be careful not to use sounds that infringe copyright, you can get into trouble and even be sued for a lot of money. Always use free and royalty-free music curtains or use curtains that you have paid for your rights.

4- The length of your podcast should be as long as you need to say what you have to say. Do not try to fill in the time to reach a specific goal because the audience will notice and is likely to get bored. It is preferable that it lasts 5 minutes and that you provide compelling content to take 30 minutes to say the same, wasting your audience's time. I like podcasts that last between 15 and 30 minutes. A podcast very well scripted, and with good music and effects can extend up to 40 minutes, more than that is not advisable.

5- When you speak, always keep the same distance between your mouth and the microphone so that the sound quality is the same during recording. One thing you can do is keep your mouth glued to the microphone filter all the time.

6- In your introduction, the idea is to tell your audience about what you are going to talk about and, if possible, include a hook to hook them, an advance of some information that you will reveal throughout the podcast, and will make the audience stay to listen.

7- At the end of your podcast, include a call to action (call to work). Whatever, for example, visit a page of your blog, buy a product, hire a service, subscribe to your list, etc.

8- Send people to your blog. In your blog, you should have a section where you upload your podcasts. On that page, you will have a summary of the essential things you have said in the podcast and some links (if possible, affiliate links).

How to monetize a podcast

Remember something significant, before thinking about any monetization method you have to earn respect and trust of your audience and get a substantial number of followers, only then can you start thinking about how to monetize your podcast.

There are several ways to monetize a podcast, and we will explore them in this chapter, but it is important to understand that podcasts are usually a very important tool to support other media, such as a blog, and are usually used more as a capture tool of audience than as a tool for direct monetization. With this clarification, let's see a little what alternatives exist to monetize a podcast.

Options to monetize a podcast:

1. Advertising

Several successful podcasters pass advertisements from

companies that pay to appear in them. While many are reluctant to include advertising in the podcast for fear of angering the listeners, the truth is that if you do your podcast as a tool to earn money and on top of your podcast adds value to the audience, it is expected that you turn to this type of monetization resources.

You should always be honest and frontal with your audience and thank the sponsor for allowing you to continue with your podcast.

2. Membership products and services

Send the audience to a specific post on your blog or website. In that post or website, you must have one or more affiliate links so that each time any of the listeners buy a product through those links, you receive a commission.

3. *Publius*

In this case, one talks about a product, service, or brand more subtly. The podcaster charges money to make a review or analysis of a particular product, service, or company trying to generate the interest of users, and therefore receives a sum of money.

4. *Construction of the personal brand*

This is a case of indirect monetization; the development of a particular brand has a significant value that later translates into higher sales of its own products or services, such as consulting.

The audience of a podcast creates significant loyalty ties with the podcaster; they trust their advice and the products that the person promotes.

5. Donations

Don't be afraid to ask your audience for help. If they get value through you, a good portion of the audience may decide to help you. You can install Paypal donation buttons on your website, and at the end of each podcast, ask listeners to remember to donate to help you with the costs of keeping the podcast active.

6. Premium Content

You can do this from Kindle, or with an iPhone or Android app. Contrary to what it seems, followers are willing to pay and collaborate with you if the proposal is excellent, and they feel that the money invested is worth it.

7. Subscription to your newsletter

Invite listeners to subscribe to your newsletter. It is an indirect monetization method, but newsletters are one of the most effective ways to monetize your followers. If your followers trust you and respect you, they will gladly accept to subscribe to your newsletter, as long as you use it correctly. For this, I recommend you read the strategy on how to create a newsletter, which explains how to build a successful newsletter.

8. *Create your products*

This option resembles some of the above, but the difference is that here, you will direct the audience to a website where your products are sold without any intermediary, increasing the sales revenue for you. It is not advisable to start developing your products until you have a significant audience.

CHAPTER 9

NETWORK MARKETING

Network marketing is based on a specific distribution principle. Many well-known companies such as Tupperware or Vorwerk work with it. Some companies promise more than they can hold. But if you get it right, it will create the basis for a passive income. We explain what exactly is behind the Network Marketing, what earning potential it brings, and how to spot black sheep in the marketplace.

What is Network Marketing? - Basics of MLM at a glance

Network marketing is a form of distribution in which products and services are sold through several independent partners. Everyone is encouraged to recruit more customers or employees. This creates a hierarchically branched distribution structure, whereby the branches established by own recruits are called downline. Their private sales and success deserve the respective seller.

For this form of distribution, there are other names such as network marketing, multi-level marketing (MLM), or structure sales. MLM points to the different levels that arise. The terms network or network marketing are all about the fact that the private system of each partner plays a vital role in sales.

The distribution partners are not employed by the companies but act as self-employed persons or as franchisees. Network marketing companies from various industries are active.

Sample calculation: How Network Marketing (MLM) works

The following example shows how compensation for network marketing could work. The assumptions are simplified to make the results easier to compare. We assume the following situation:

- Five levels
- Fixed product prices
- Each person (except the lower level) has recruited three distribution partners.
- Sales by direct sales per person: 300 €
- 20% commission for direct sales
- 1% Pro-rata commission on the revenue of each subordinate level

Legend:

Nof: Number of distributors

SRPL: Sales revenue per level (€)

CFHL: Commission for the highest level (€)

Level 1   1 (NoF)   300 (SRPL)   60
(CFHL) (direct commission: 20%)

Level 2   3 (NoF)   900 (SRPL)   9
(CFHL) (indirect commission: 1%)

Level 3   9 (NoF)   2700 (SRPL)   27
(CFHL) (indirect commission: 1%)

Level 4   81 (NoF)   24,300 (SRPL)   243
(CFHL) (indirect commission: 1%)

Level 5   6561 (NoF)   1968300 (SRPL) 19,683
(CFHL) (indirect commission: 1%)

In the example, you can see that at level 5, lower-level commission shares have a more significant percentage of earnings than direct sales commissions. This effect intensifies even in the higher levels. If recruiting new employees brings significantly more money than selling the products, this indicates a snowball system banned in Germany.

MLM companies try to prevent the emergence of such a system by setting limits. If you can only earn money at a limited number of levels, this is called a depth limit. With a **width limit, the number of branches of this tree hierarchy is reduced.**

The example presented is just one of many ways that compensation could be regulated. Sometimes a

commission is paid on every level so that the products are always more expensive. Most compensation plans are not that easy either. Often bonuses play a role, and you get from a fixed sales limit an individual status or points are distributed.

However, all models of merit have one thing in common: they earn money from the recruited sales partners and their activities. This has a very motivating effect.

Earnings opportunities in network marketing - and what the passive income is MLM companies often advertise with high earning potential. It is already justified in the system that not everyone can reach these maximum sums. Most people consider network marketing as a sideline. Make sure that you do not require a high initial investment, training fees, or licensing fees, and that you do not have to take minimum quantities. Because then there is also a risk of loss.

The earnings opportunities in network marketing vary from 0 Euro per month to 4, 5, or even 6-figure monthly income. Such network marketers, who are at the upper level of the distribution structure, often generate millions of dollars in monthly revenue.

The earnings opportunities in network marketing depend mainly on the following points:

- Deductibility of products (market saturation, value for money)

- The compensation plan of the company

- Scope of your own downline

- Motivation and sales talent

Since you benefit from the sales of your downline, it is a kind of passive income, similar to affiliate marketing. This means you can earn money even without your purchases. However, in some companies, you have the function of a consultant for the low levels, who may also provide training. Depending on the compensation model, however, you may lose your status and thus earning opportunities if sales are insufficient. In this respect, some compensation models are only conditionally passive income. You should check this in advance.

Multi-Level Marketing: Benefits and Disadvantages

To decide if network marketing is right for you, you need to know the pros and cons of these systems. It also depends on personal preferences, whether one feels a quality as positive or negative. The following points speak for this distribution form.

Advantages:

- Chance of a guaranteed passive income
- Open time-management
- Diversified
- Contact with people

Several factors need to be considered critically. How strong these depend on the individual company.

Disadvantage:

- Partly unrealistic promises

- Stressing personal relationships through sales activities in the private sphere

- Aggressive advertising methods (not with all companies)

- Sometimes close to the snowball system

- Corporate risk

2 Top Network Marketing Companies in 2019

Companies in various industries work according to the principle of network marketing. Some have been successful for a long time. Others are only establishing themselves. Three of the most well-known companies active in Germany are Juice Plus +, Tupperware.

Sales are based on the principle of network marketing, whereby the distribution partners conclude a franchise agreement. The task is to attract customers. The company ships the products to these after they have ordered online.

- *Tupperware: A classic among the MLM*

Classic Tupperware products are the kitchen and

household items made of plastic, such as the famous Tupperware. Since the year 2000, cosmetics and care products have also been part of the product range. The sale takes place mainly via Tupperpartys in private households.

The first product of the US Company, the wonder bowl, came in 1946 on the market. In 1948, the idea of Tupperware Home Parties came into being, laying the foundation for network marketing. In Germany, about 70,000 consultants work for the company.

- *Juice Plus +: network marketing company from the USA*

Juice Plus + is a brand of the US company National Safety Associates and in the US since 1993 on the market. The main product is capsules with fruit and vegetable powder. Diet shakes and similar products are part of the assortment. For some years now, Juice Plus + has also been distributed in Europe, with the company benefiting from the boom in nutritional supplements.

Be part of a reputable network marketing company - that's how it works

Maybe you have been to various sales parties or been advertised in another way by acquaintances or strangers for the cooperation in a structured sales. Of course, MLM distributors have an interest in expanding they're downline. However, you should not make such decisions lightly, even as a matter of courtesy. Follow these steps if you can imagine working in network marketing.

How to find a suitable network marketing company:

1. Inform yourself Internet.

2. If you have chosen a few favorites, have a look at their website. Is the information transparent enough?

3. Check the price-performance ratio of the products.

4. Search online for experiences. Unfortunately, some MLM companies use questionable methods.

5. Search for someone who has achieved excellent results in that network and contact them (Facebook and LinkedIn could be a great resource for you)

6. The next steps vary from company to company. It may be that someone answers you that you should attend training or that you can start immediately. Follow the individual instructions.

You Should Also Know About Network Marketing

In the past, network marketing (MLM) has repeatedly come under fire. It is not the system itself that should be called into question, but the methods of some MLM companies. The following criticisms will help you distinguish acute from dubious business models.

Pyramid schemes

Ponzi schemes are considered fraud in Germany. Typical of this is that a few people earn a lot of money at the expense of many others. These systems cannot work permanently. An unregulated structure distribution would develop into a pyramid scheme. The MLM companies prevent this, for example, by limiting the downline.

Unrealistic promises

This cause for criticism is, unfortunately, prevalent. Many companies advertise with income that few employees will reach. With publications of the real merit numbers, most network marketing companies hold back.

Bad value for money

The distribution structure of network marketing usually causes higher costs than the traditional way of wholesale and retail. As a result, compared to commercially available similar goods, the products are generally more expensive. Often, therefore, the customers and distribution partners are taught that this is particularly high quality. That is to be examined in the individual case.

Aggressive or manipulative customer or partner acquisition

From unwanted contact to permanent offers to sect-like structures - with some MLM companies, you do not feel right. Stay away from aggressive sales methods. If you apply them yourself in your environment, it can permanently damage your social relationships.

Inadequate consultancy skills

For the sale of household items, candles, or jewelry, you need no specialized knowledge. It is enough if you know the assortment. Things are different in the areas of finance and health. Do you prefer, in this case, the company, one at its distribution partner's appropriate training, require or support them?

MLM companies choose carefully and make money

As a distribution partner in network marketing, you can build up a partially passive income. Whether it is suitable for the main job depends on the company and the success of your sales. As a rule, the MLM is more of a sideline business.

Network marketing companies of various industries are active. When selecting, make sure that you can identify with both the products and the company, and that this is a serious business, for example, without a pyramid scheme.

CHAPTER 10

KINDLE PUBLISHING

It seems that selling on Amazon is very fashionable, whatever it is. You can sell your products, do dropshipping, sell on Amazon as an affiliate, or sell kindle books. The idea is to make money with Amazon in all or some of the options where you can choose.

Since there are different ways to make money with Amazon, and it is understood that each of them has a different format, in this chapter, I will focus only on selling Kindle Ebooks. But before continuing, I would like to give a preview of the other formulas that you can use with Amazon.

- **Sell Kindle Ebooks**

It is necessary to clarify that this chapter does not pretend to be a tutorial of the sale on Amazon. It doesn't even pretend to be a recommendation to sell books on the Kindle program, and it's just about telling, in my way, my own experiences with this program.

I had already known Amazon for a long time, in fact, I participated in several of its affiliate programs, practically from all countries, I have already paid a few times, and even when it is clear that they pay, it is not enough to affirm it.

Well, in this case, I will talk about the Kindle program, that is, sell e-books on Amazon. I want to tell you about my experience with everything I have been learning, the most important information I know, and some other details.

Although I already have experience in writing reports, articles, guides, tutorials, I needed to leap to something more advanced, creating an electronic book that could be sold, which is not easy.

A few months ago, I entered the Kindle program, and I just had a clear idea, I had to try. So throw me and publish my first book. I am not a writer, I am very far from being one, and however, I think I can transform my experiences into more great books with information that can be useful for many people.

And this is one of the essential points for any book that claims to be sold. On Amazon or any other site, you must at least give a minimum of service through information.

With all this process, I have had many "headaches" since it was not exactly as I expected. My first book was only right about the content, at least it was what I thought, which is not small, but there are many other factors to keep in mind that not only the content.

First steps with Kindle

1) Entering the Amazon Kindle program is easy, an email, credit or debit card, Payoneer, confirmation, you select the continent where you want to sell and ready, later it can serve you for other services such as Amazon Fba, for example.

2) Selling your book on Amazon is also relatively easy, you have to fill in the information they ask for, upload your cover, upload the book in Word and they convert it to you in Kindle format, that is, Epub, Mobi, etc., to that can be read in the readers...

Following all these steps, you are already in the Amazon Kindle program. Now let's see the details of each of the parts. I will try to be as transparent as possible...

Note: The final step to complete the previous series is to find potential customers who can be ultimate buyers of your product or book, and this step is not as simple as it seems.

Technical details to sell kindle

Once you are clear that you want to sell kindle on Amazon and you enter the publication, you begin to see some features that can be important if you do not consider them. For example, seeing your book in Word format is not the same as seeing it converted into an Epub; it has nothing to do with it.

For your Kindle book to have a professional-looking minimum, it must meet a few requirements, which, if you are not used to it, maybe difficult for you to reach a "distant world." It's about knowing how to prepare your ebook in a Word document so that it can be converted into Epub and at the same time, save some details of the look you would like.

If you believe it in Word format and do not respect the minimum requirements, surely the texts will be decompensated, the images super compressed, and it will be difficult even to read. Of course, Amazon offers you plenty of information about it, and the problem is reading it and putting it into practice. I know we are all in a hurry for many things; with these issues, you must be very patient.

There is also a lot of information on the internet on the subject, some more technical than the others, but I have not yet found a complete Amazon Kindle tutorial because I understand that it is very complicated to offer, including all the details.

The basic thing is to know Word...

You should know how to format texts, insert different functionalities, how to put the indexes, spaces between lines, the recommended fonts, the ideal size, etc. Kindle images are another big problem, so if you're not very used to it, it's better than the limits.

Typefaces for Kindle formats

To date, the formats I know of the font to use are these; Arial, Baskerville, Caecilia, Courier, Georgia, Helvetica, Lucida Sans Unicode, Palatine, Times New Roman, Trebuchet, Verdana.

The font size for Kindle

The volume also matters in the fonts you use for your Kindle book if you do not want to see it unbalanced, of course, there may be some difference between the fiction or the "non-fiction" books, when the size 11 or 12 is typically used for the first, for the second you can use up to 13 0 14, of course, this is only a recommendation.

The spaces between lines are also important, for Kindle fiction books it is not usually used and for "non-fiction" Kindle, variations between 0.5 to 1.5 are used more frequently, titles must be highlighted, and at the same time they must be adjusted, the description with smaller size and the rest of the justified text or aligned to the left.

- **Kindle images**

The images are another big problem of the Kindle readers, and in case you did not know, an image does not look the same in Kindle Fire HD, Kindle Fire HDX or Kindle Fire HDX 8.9. This is because, if you use the Kindle program converter, it automatically compresses all of them; in other words, all the images that pass 127kb will be compressed, affecting their appearance and resolution.

From this we can deduce several things, the first that we must use images in Jpg and edit them in independent editors such as Photoshop or similar editors to save the maximum resolution, the second is to adjust the sizes since the program only allows up to 600x400px at the most, the third is to prepare in Word regarding the images to achieve the desired effect.

Note: If you are not attentive, your images will not be seen in sure readers or will look very small or unbalanced, the solution to this problem is to be careful in adjusting the format that Word incorporates by default.

To insert images from Word with the ideal format for Kindle, we add the image frequently and then, within the image, select "size and position," uncheck the "Lock aspect ratio" box and reset, in the next picture, you look better.

In this step, if the image is enormous, you can get careless in Word, do not worry, this is not important since the Kindle converter will adjust it directly, in this way, your Kindle Ebook will fit you a little better, and it will look more professional.

Note: I am not an expert, I only tell my own experience it is all that I have been learning during the last months since I decided to enter the Kindle program.

What to sell on Amazon Kindle

Well, I get tired of so much technical detail, which is not easy, it is rather quite complicated, anyway, let's go to what interests, selling in Amazon kindle is secure, LIE, as in any program or product, it is more complicated than it seems.

Although I am not an expert in writing, I honestly do not even think about it, I can say that in other aspects I am, as far as I can, I have been selling for a few years, and in this field, I know what I am talking about.

On the other hand, to write, if you do not know very well how to do it, you can always hire someone in places like fiver or similar, however, to make money with Amazon, you will not get it just by publishing your book and sitting down to wait.

Regardless of the content contained in your book, it is still a product that needs sales marketing, and this means that you must "move it," but let's go in parts...

You can sell Ebooks of anything

For those of us who are dedicated to marketing, we can sell techniques on this or that, systems on how to make money, how to create a blog or a website, how to use this or that tool. Everything related to the word "Like" works in all niches, "how to train a dog," "how to create a blog," "how to swim on all fours," anything serves to sell kindle on Amazon.

- **The trick...**

If there is, it consists of looking for content related to what we try to sell on Amazon in kindle format, then develop it, layout it and put it on sale. Of course, we are talking about "non-fiction" books since the others are another story full of many details that I will not enter.

- **Any doubts**

From all this information, some questions may arise, how many pages our book should have, how many words, with or without images, what price to put, among many others. For the information I have, with a book between 25 and 40 pages and between 7,000 and 15,000 words, it would be enough to give it as valid, the prices are relative to your claims from $0.99.

How to make money with Amazon Kindle

After explaining some details about how to create your Kindle Ebook and publish it on Amazon, it's time to sell to make money on Amazon with your books. And we are not talking about how to make money with a single book, the idea of this section is to indicate that not everything stops in a single book.

To earn money with Amazon, you will not get it with a single Ebook, not even with a unique niche or micro-niche, at least this is my case. When I started with my first Kindle book, the days went by, and I didn't get results.

After a while, I looked for more information on the subject, and among everything I learned I have a sure thing, I had to expand my area of action. I had a lot of desire, useful information, and enough knowledge of ebook preparation. So I decided to try it with other niches, and that is when I got some results.

The steps to make money with Amazon Kindle:

1. Create your first book and promote it as much as you can.

2. Create your second Ebook from the same niche and the third, fourth, etc.

3. Don't stop around, create Kindle books from other niches, if you don't know about them, hire someone to believe them.

4. Set goals to create, for example, 1 per week, 4 per month, 60 per year.

5. Take care of the details of each book, especially the covers and content structure.

6. Think about using Amazon advertising.

7. If you want more sales to look at the option of the lowest price, you will undoubtedly sell more...

Selling Kindle on Amazon can be profitable if you take it seriously, this should not fit the slightest doubt since the platform puts at your disposal the necessary means to publish your books very quickly. Also, it has the most extensive library in the world, and it is these details that can benefit you taking advantage of its full potential.

If you already know what I am talking about, you will surely agree with me, if you have not yet started to create and publish your Ebook in Amazon Kindle, now is a good time to do it and see for yourself the results.

If you don't know where to start, you can do it by creating your Amazon Kindle account and experimenting. If you are wrong, do not worry, you try again if your books are not sold try to improve them or make different ones, the idea is NEVER TO GIVE UP.

If you do not know what to sell, you can enter Amazon and search for those themes or categories that interest you collecting ideas. Then you look for information, complete, improvements, and turn it into an Ebook for Kindle.

You can also use tools to sell on Amazon, which there are and very good as KindleSpy that helps you find the bestselling books in all formats and categories. The good thing about this tool is that in a few clicks, you can have privileged information at your fingertips.

If you don't know how to write, look for people to help you, you have many places to find FreeLancers willing to work with you. The forums are a good start at low cost, that is, you have no excuses not to try if your idea is to make money with Amazon kindle.

Who knows if in a while, you become an Amazon Best Seller and you become famous.

CHAPTER 11

DEVELOP YOUR APP

Those who want to develop an app often think that they only have to generate enough downloads to be able to earn money with the project. In this chapter, we always point out that you must have a strong monetization strategy to prevail in the app stores. Because even about user numbers, successful apps often do not generate any sales at all - but at the same time enormous costs.

One reason that many customers underestimate the difficulty of ROI is a flawed cost estimate: many people think to have an app developed costs a few hundred dollars! Of course, it's nothing like it. Many apps that we use every day have cost well over $50,000 in the first development step alone. Added to this are the running costs, the costs for the further development and expenses for administrative tasks for the operator of a mobile application. If you want to plan your project professionally right from the beginning, you should consider in detail how high the app development costs are. But we do not want to discourage you from this chapter. A professional project can be very profitable. As? Keep reading, and get to know the most important strategies!

Monetization of free applications

Free app with in-app purchases

The first model is one of the most popular: The download of the app is generally open for each user. Especially for Android apps, this is usually recommended. The provider earns money through the opportunity for users to buy something within the app. Here are many different products conceivable. From the purchase of a paid premium version of the free basic app (freemium model) on the purchase of products (M-commerce) to payment systems through the app at parking machines or the box office, the provider is endless ways open.

Example: A 3D mobile game is free and offers a basic version of the game. The user can play the first three levels for free and is then delivered to buy more levels. Instead of new standards, the user could also buy individual items (new weapons, extra lives, etc.). It is also conceivable that he can play the whole game, but must endorse advertising. By downloading the paid ad-free version, the provider earns money.

This monetization strategy can be very successful. But the provider must be aware that he must plan the purchase well. If the offer is placed incorrectly or the basic version is not attractive enough, the shot will backfire because the users will not recognize the value of the app.

Free App with In-App Advertisement

The ability to earn money with a free app by showing banner ads, videos, or pop-ups in the application is well known to most. You can demand payment from the advertisers. Often, a pay-per-click system is used.

The problem here is that the mobile app provider often advertises at the expense of the user experience. One can counteract this with the skillful placement of the advertising content.

Much more problematic is that the analysis of the numbers shows that advertising is rarely really worthwhile. Many advertisers have already noticed that only a few users click on the banners and videos. And who clicks on it, the landing page often leaves after a second again, because only inadvertently clicked on the advertising. It is, therefore, tough to achieve marketing success, which, of course, the advertisers are not willing to pay a large sum for each click.

Freemium App

We have already explained the freemium model above. However, this model is so successful and popular that we would like to take a closer look at it here.

A freemium app is nothing more than a free app that you can upgrade for a fee. There are no limits to the possibilities. The best way to explain them is with examples:

There are two versions of the same app. One version provides the basis. Here are some things to consider: Advertising is shown, the speed is lower, some features are not available, there is only the English version, etc. The second version fixes the "error" of the first: It is ad-free, the performance is better, the user can use all functions unrestricted, the language can be set, etc., etc.

Items can be bought in the app. In many apps, the user uses a variety of items to solve tasks. However, only limited items are available by paying a minimal amount but can be purchased additionally. The easiest way is that there is an internal currency in the app (buttons), which can be exchanged for real money. A little tip on the edge: It has a psychologically positive if you get a lot of buttons with little money. So 1 $ = 1000 buttons, instead of 1$ = 10 buttons.

There are also some apps where you can create an account for free, whereby the number of accounts per user is limited. However, if the user wants to create more accounts, he has to download a paid version. If you cannot imagine why the user should do this, you will get two examples: In a football manager game, the user has an account and thus participates in a private league. However, he can only create a team like that. If he had multiple accounts, he could create different groups, join various associations, and use the app longer.

Another example is payroll accounting programs. On PCs, you can create your payroll for free with a basic version. But if you also want to create accounts for clients, you have to buy a premium version, to register multiple users. Of course, you can also transfer this to mobile devices.

It is important to emphasize that this list is far from complete. You can vary the incentives for the user, or even combine different models. So a basic version with ads and a paid premium version is an app with in-app purchases and in-app advertisement, but at the same time follows the freemium approach.

Free trial software

This model is easy to understand. The user can download the app for free and use it for two weeks, one month, or any other specified time. Subsequently, however, he must install a paid version if he wants to continue using the mobile app.

This model is very commonly used in software for the PC. However, it is scarce to find it in mobile apps. Nonetheless, applications, especially in the business sector, are also conceivable for mobile devices.

The advantage is that users can test them completely risk-free, which can be a positive marketing effect that can be achieved. Tip: IF the user decides to pay after the test phase, he will be satisfied. That's when you should ask him for a review on the App Store! On the other hand, avoid asking users for a rating that decides against it.

Develop a paid app

Of course, mobile apps that cost money to download are downloaded less frequently, such as free apps. And you need thousands of downloads to cover the development costs. The most common mistake made when developing paid apps is a simple miscalculation. Again, I'll explain this with an example:

Not so long ago, I received a business plan from a customer who testified. The customer assumes development costs of $10,000 and running costs of $5,000 / year. He needs at least 15,000 downloads in the first year because he wants to offer his app for $1 in the App Store. What would happen if 15,000 users purchased the app? Of course, you spend $15,000. But does the provider, therefore, create the ROI? No! Because of every purchase made by the app stores, the operators of the marketplaces keep about 1/3 of the money! The customer lacks $5,000, although he would have achieved his goals, which would be worthy of all honor.

It is, therefore, challenging to cover development costs in the long term; especially if you want to offer the app at fair prices. But it is by no means impossible.

However, it is existential for the user to know that your app is worth paying for. This means that the app is so relevant to a niche that users cannot help but buy the app, or your brand is or becomes so well known that customers know what your app can do.

Of course, it is also essential in this context that this strategy is much more promising for iOS than for Android. In Google Play, paid apps are the absolute rarity, and few users are willing to pay for a download.

Other forms of profitable mobile apps

Some providers of apps do not want to earn money directly with an app. Large corporations are often only for image reasons to develop an app. To increase your reach and to achieve a marketing effect, a global player can sometimes develop a very complex app and invest vast amounts of money. The ROI takes place indirectly for them, in that the app appeals to potential customers, improves the image, or reaches a new target group.

There is a particular case with so-called non-profit projects. Here, an organization wants to achieve a goal that has nothing to do with monetary or other material benefits. The purpose of the apps, on the other hand, is to make people aware of environmental protection, to educate children and adolescents, or to educate society.

Yeeply's tips for your success

After showing you how to make money from apps, we want to give you some tips along the way that we always recommend to our customers.

Think of the taxes and duties

Unfortunately, some providers run a project for the first

time "on their account" and are surprised that gross is not equal to the net. A particular case is that used services must be obtained from other countries. Also, remember that there might be different VAT rates. Also, note the mentioned charges that you have to pay to the app stores, etc.

Choose the right model for your app

Not every monetization strategy fits any mobile app. Before you develop your app, you should think about which model fits your app, your target audience, and your goals. At this point, you can also do pure market research: tell ten people roughly about your idea and ask you what the people would be willing to pay. Even the development departments of large companies proceed in this way.

Do not ask for basic options

A common mistake is to ask the user for money features that he can use in the basic version. If the user does not get real added value, he feels cheated.

With extra features set off from the competition

To be able to develop a successful app, the unique selling proposition is an important element. You can use additional paid features to set yourself apart from competing apps. On the other hand, you can also look for what the competition demands money for and offer that free!

A mobile app is not a website

Clear! You can also have a responsive website developed instead of an app. But anyone who owns a website and wants to develop an app must be aware of the peculiarities of mobile applications and not just be able to offer a website optimized for the surface. In the case of mobile apps, the effect of banner advertising, performance issues, user behavior, development costs, etc. are quite different than web pages. Therefore, your monetization strategy must be specially adapted to your app.

We sincerely hope that you now have an idea of how mobile apps can become profitable.

CHAPTER 12

HOW TO MAKE MONEY ON YOUTUBE?

Consider the following:

We won't tell you what content you can create on YouTube, but we have a responsibility to do the right thing for our viewers, creators, and advertisers. If you are part of the YouTube Partner Program, you can earn money through the platform, and therefore, you will be subject to higher standards.

To make sure you reward good creators, we first review your channel to accept you on the YouTube Partner Program. We also regularly review the gutters to ensure that you comply with our policies and guidelines.

Ways to earn money in the YouTube Partner Program

You can make money on YouTube through the following functions:

- **Advertising revenue:** Earn revenue from graphics, overlay, and video ads.
- **Channel Memberships:** Your members make recurring monthly payments in exchange for the exclusive benefits you offer.

145

- **Product library:** Fans can explore and buy the official merchandising that stands out on your playback pages.
- **Super chat:** Fans pay to make their messages stand out on broadcast chats.
- **YouTube Premium Revenue:** Get a share of the subscription rate of YouTube Premium users when they watch your content.

Each function has its eligibility requirements (in addition to subscribers and view counts). You may not be able to activate a specific service if our reviewers believe that your channel or video is not suitable. These additional limits exist for two main reasons. The most important is that we must comply with legal requirements in all areas where the function is available. The other purpose is that we must ensure that the channels have the necessary context (which, many times, means that we need more content) to evaluate them, and thus be able to reward good creators.

Keep in mind that we continuously review the channels to ensure that the content complies with our policies.

Minimum eligibility requirements to activate monetization functions

Keep in mind that each service has its own needs. Some of them may not be available due to local legal requirements.

Once we accept you in the YouTube Partner Program, you may have access to the following monetization features:

Ad revenue:

•   Be over 18 or have a legal guardian over 18 who can handle your payments through AdSense

•   Create content that meets our content requirements for advertisers

Channel Memberships:

•   Being over 18 years

•   Have more than 30,000 subscribers

•   Not have any warning for breach of the Community Guidelines

Product library:

•   Being over 18 years

•   Have more than 10,000 subscribers

•   Not have any advice for violation of the Community Guidelines

Super chat:

•   Being over 18 years

•   Live in a country or region where Super chat is available

YouTube Premium earnings:

• Have a YouTube Premium subscriber watch the content you created

CHAPTER 13

PASSIVE INCOME WITH P2P LOANS

Digitalization is not only changing our everyday lives, but it is also revolutionizing the financial market and entire industries. This includes the banking industry, which has undergone an impressive metamorphosis in recent centuries anyway. However, traditional lending remains one of the main pillars of the banking industry. Banks have long had a monopoly on this source of income. However, this could be given a whole new twist by the impressive development of peer-to-peer lending (P2P). Peer-to-peer lending is hardly known in this country. P2P Credit offers an opportunity to combine high returns with a thoroughly human character, even beating the banks.

What are P2P loans?

P2P loans are direct loans from a private individual to a private individual. Transactions are handled through digital platforms, eliminating the need for banks (and their sometimes horrendous fees) for the distribution process. Like everywhere else in the economy, lending is governed by the basic principle of supply and demand. In many countries, there is a high demand for credit, but the offer often leaves much to be desired.

Here we are strongly blinded by the low-interest rate strategy of the major central banks around the world. We assume that our very low-interest rates would have to be found everywhere in Europe. While that for refinancing is correct to some extent, this bill falls apart when looking at the use of loans to individuals in many economically less participating in European countries, eg. For example, in the Balkans, it is hardly possible as a private person to obtain bank loans below 10 percent interest. While a mortgage with 10 percent interest in Lithuania or Spain means good business for the borrower, in Germany, we can only achieve such returns through high-risk activity. This creates a situation from which both sides can benefit.

How P2P loans work in 3 steps

1. The first step is to open an account on one or more platforms that best complement your preferences. Then you can deposit there using your investor ID, money by bank transfer.

2. Then you can give your money as credits. This can be done manually by analyzing the loans and borrowers and deciding whether you want to put your money there or by using the auto-invest feature.

3. If you want to have your money back one day, you can transfer it to your account. If you're going to liquidate more loans, you have two options. You can wait until the loans have been repaid (interest and repayment) and pay you the money. For this, you must deactivate the auto-

invest function. But you can also sell your loans on the secondary market and get your money faster. However, this often goes hand in hand with losses!

The most critical terms in P2P investing

Bestinvest: After you have logged in, you must first transfer money to the respective platform. Once it has arrived there, it can be lent.

Reinvest, or Autoinvest stands for automated investment. Your "winnings" (interest and repayment installments) are automatically reinvested with the minimum amount of financing you set, thereby generating a compound interest effect. Exactly that and the accompanying time savings should be the goal of passive investing! Of course, you can also choose your loans. But that means a lot of busy work and thus time, which I prefer to save as a lazy dog.

Financing sum: Only if the entire amount of the loan request can be collected (the loan is adequately capitalized), the lending comes off. That's why I love the auto-invest feature. Otherwise, too often, I would have to spend too much time working on bad credit and looking for new investment opportunities.

Score / Rating / Credit Rating: There is a rating for the borrower made by financial rating firms. However, each marketplace uses different agencies for this purpose. Based on individual vital figures, a first credit check of the borrower is thus carried out. This is important to be able to assess the risk of investments.

Loan subscribers are those who originally brokered the loans. A better term would, therefore, be loan providers. They then sell the loans to investors via the platforms.

Issuer Risk: This refers to the risk of bankruptcy of many P2P platforms. Because should the operator of the platform become insolvent, your entire money could be gone. For this not to happen, the money invested in the operator platforms is often covered by insolvency law. An insolvency administrator or so-called liquidator then take care of any problems. Also, your uninvested money is secured up to the deposit insurance of the respective country. A 100 percent guarantee that you get your money back in case of cases is not!

Delay: Many P2P beginners hit their hands over their heads for the first time at the latest when they notice early delinquencies by borrowers. This is not so bad at first, as several default months are often paid at one go. Also, you will receive additional default interest for the default period!

Default: The significant risk of P2P loans is that borrowers can default. That's why it's so important to spread your investment as broadly as possible!

Liquidity: Depending on how long you set the repayment terms in which you are willing to invest, the lower your cash. However, you can always sell your investments in the secondary market (usually against discounts). So you want to ensure high liquidity, you should only invest in loans that have a low (remaining) loan period.

Parameters: Several factors are important to you or your risk-return ratio in personal loans. Depending on how you choose it, you either have a high risk with high return or low risk with a low back.

LTV: The loan to value is the lending rate (lending value) or the cost of the loan against the deposited security (e.g., a house or car). The calculation is simple, and only the loan size has to be divided by the value size. The higher the credit taken about the value, the riskier the investment!

Portfolio value (aspired) should always be set higher so that the money is reinvested automatically and does not remain in the account.

Interest rate: Can be customized by you on most platforms. One thing is clear: the higher the interest rate set by you, the higher the default risk and vice versa.

Primary Market and Secondary Market: On the secondary market, you can buy loans that other people sell. In the secondary market, you can often find loans that have already advanced in the dunning process or just those that someone wants to get rid of because he wants to liquidate his investment. You can also sell loans from you with a markup or discount. Some people specialize in this active form of investment and report astronomical returns. After all, profits can be made immediately. However, this not only increases the risk, but also the time investment required of you!

Buyback Guarantee: On some platforms, e.g., B. Mintos, you can invest in loans with buyback guarantee. This has the advantage that the platform, the loan, if a specific default (e.g., 60 days +) incurred by one of your borrowers, buys back from you. For this period, you even get interested and interest on arrears.

Yield Calculation Systems: Each platform performs its calculation of returns. Therefore, a comparison is often possible only by its estimates. All you need is the following data: 1. Your exact deposits and withdrawals on your marketplace with date; 2. Your current account balance. So you have a little work with it, I have designed a simple Excel spreadsheet, Keep in mind, however, that the calculation of the internal interest rate (XIRR) is significant only after one year, so if you have your capital already working for you for some time.

My tips for smart P2P investing

1. Do not spend more than 5% of your assets on a single platform. You usually have a threefold risk on P2P platforms. Platforms, lenders, and borrowers may fail! Therefore, be sure to diversify across multiple platforms to reduce platform risk.

2. Stick to the unwritten law of not investing more than 1% of your portfolio value in a single project or loan. Diversify your credit, so by z. For example, spend one percent of your total investment on the platform per loan (at least $ 5). In this way, you ensure the broadest possible diversification. Even smaller denominations usually reduce the risk, but then also increases your administrative expenses exponentially. Besides, we want to generate passive and non-active income. For a degree of diversification, one percent is sufficient! So you do not have to strive for maximum diversification by spreading the minimum investment! However, I also collect your own experience here.

3. Adjust your chosen parameters regularly.

4. Taxes: Get the tax office confirmed that you pay your taxes in Germany. Otherwise, you have to pay them abroad (e.g., Latvia), but they will not get back! You can download the form from the Federal Central Tax Office. Fill it out, send it to your tax office and wait for the confirmation.

5. Enter a more extensive portfolio size, as your currently invested amount, so that you come through the car investment on the target amount. Otherwise, this mechanism will stop too soon and may not reinvest!

6. I personally only invested in the platforms that offer the auto-invest feature. I do not feel like spending actively, but want to achieve passive income!

7. Do not worry if loans fail. As long as the return on average is right, that does not matter and is reasonable! In this country, borrowers are also out, and residual sums have to be written off. Remember that we are primarily interested in interest rates. So, if our investment is low (small minimum investment), then we can have the investment back within a year through the interest rates. Everything that comes later is practically a bonus (+ amortization at the end). So you also learn a bit about how the traditional lending business at banks works.

8. If you have an online presence or social media channels, you can increase your return through affiliate links of the respective platforms. I also use this way. If you register for one of the following links for a P2P platform, I will receive a small commission for this. For you, this has no disadvantages, but for me, it is additional support.

CHAPTER 14

TRADING

Can you make money from trading? - In this chapter, I'll give you an answer from my personal experience. I explain to you about the opportunities and risks in the markets. What can one expect from trading, and what is impossible? I will give you a checklist to maximize your profits. - Inform yourself in detail before you start the stock market trading!

Making money on the computer with just a few clicks sounds very easy and is possible with the trading and the financial markets. However, it is assumed that a trader can take certain risks to make any profit. What many beginners and advanced people do not realize is that a trader has to be an intelligent risk manager!

The risk has to be managed intelligently, and when it is about to be taken out of the market as soon as possible. Only those who control their losses and can accept them will end up being a successful trader.

Short overview:

- Making money with trading is 100% possible

- Without risk, you will not be able to make money on the stock market

- Knowledge about the markets and the trade are possible

- Most importantly, it's your own risk to manage

Trading Experience: There Are Only 2 Options

What comes in addition to the easy work on the computer money in a few clicks is that there are only two options on the stock market: It is either only upwards (long) or down (short). You only have these two options as a trader: buy or sell. Unlike other jobs or jobs, this small range of options is a huge advantage.

The same applies to the trader. This can either only make a profit or a loss. The exception here is the breakpoint. This means that there is no price difference in the opening and closing of the trading position.

In summary, the whole thing sounds simple at first. The rules are transparent and unchangeable. In principle, a regular trade is carried out here. Traders buy an asset at a low price and try to get rid of that asset at a higher price, the profit and loss results from the price difference.

The advantages and disadvantages

To earn money with trading, you also need to know the pros and cons, which have been addressed in the upper part of the text a bit. Get a good overview in the table below:

ADVANTAGES:

- No physical effort

- With a few clicks, you make money

- Unlimited profits are possible

- Fast and long-term profits are possible.

DISADVANTAGES:

- You can lose money (high risk)

- Elaborate and continuous learning is required

Make more money with derivatives and levers

Thanks to new financial products (leveraged derivatives) and the service of some brokers, traders can now make even more profit in the markets. Also, trading with small capital is entirely possible and can lead to high earnings through correct speculation. We are talking about trading in derivatives, which in many cases, are traded with high leverage.

The advantage of derivatives is that they are created for any size of capital. It is possible to start with just a few cents and increase the money. The derivative is always derived to a base value. You can invest in any number of markets. The broker allows you to work with a lever.

The lever is a loan or additional capital for the trader. With a smaller margin, a more significant position size may be traded. The risk is covered by a stop loss or a margin call. The lever increases the potential gain or loss. Special security precautions avoid debt or extreme losses for traders.

Summary of Chances in Trading:

- Trading is possible with any size of capital

- The use of a lever allows more money to win or lose

- You can invest in countless markets

- Various tools and debts can secure the risk

Checklist: Making Money with Trading

In the following list, I will give you different tips to make the maximum profit with trading. This is especially suitable for beginners to prepare for the markets. Use this checklist to learn step by step how to make money from trading.

I focus on avoiding losses and maximizing profits. Only if you understand these two control factors in trading can you make a long-term profit? Trade in the financial markets does not necessarily have to be complicated. You must have the correct information.

1. Which markets are best for profit?

Before trading, the trader should think about the markets. Which markets would he like to trade and at what time? In the text below, I will give you a brief overview of the markets and their difficulties. For most traders, it is best to use Forex and CFDs (Contracts for Difference). This allows you to invest almost in virtually all markets very quickly at small fees.

But before that, you have to say that you can make money with every market. Traders usually have specific preferences. Try out different markets yourself:

- **Forex (currencies):** is the most liquid market in the world. The volatility (strength of the price movement) is correspondingly low. These markets are very suitable for beginners. You can invest with minimal capital and leverage. Also, trading fees are meager. In forex trading, you can catch prominent trends and react to business news.

- **Stock indices (Dax, S & P500):** are a basket of different stocks shown in an index. Almost every country has such an index. CFD (contract for difference) can trade inexpensive these markets. They are also very suitable for beginners.

- **Cryptocurrencies:** are highly volatile and involve a higher risk than the other markets presented. This market is driven by various news and hype. Every investor should think twice about investing here. The movements of these markets are mostly irrational and incomprehensible.

- **Stocks:** can also be traded very quickly with a broker. Even speculate on falling prices with a short sale. Stocks do not always have to be extremely liquid. Ideally, corporate news can be traded here, and global economic trends caught.

- **Commodities:** are driven by global economic development. Political decisions can also influence the courses. Products can also be easily traded CFD and leverage long or short.

2. Choose the right trading platform and broker

The selection of the broker plays a significant role in your earnings. Many beginners often choose the wrong provider with too high fees because they follow advertising promises. The number of trading fees can significantly reduce your profits. Prices are a critical issue, especially in short-term trading.

Also, the trading platform should work stably. The broker should have no disconnects and give you an excellent market execution. In the following points and tables, you will be recommended by me tested and trusted brokers. From more than five years of trading experience in the financial markets, I have compared the best.

The provider should necessarily have an official license for the financial markets. Brokers without a license can, in many cases, be considered fraudulent. Also, you should be able to test the Anbeiter free, to get an insight into the trade and the markets.

Factors for a good provider selection:

- Regulation And License

- Free Demo Account With Virtual Credit

- Small Fees

- No Hidden Costs

- Stable Trading Platform

- Wide Choice Of Markets

- Fast And Professional support

3. Deposit and withdrawal with the trading account

Are you ready to invest real money? (Assuming you have practiced trading in the demo account) Do you feel secure in trading? - Then you can make your first deposit into the trading account. The sediment at the above-recommended providers works very fast and uncomplicated.

Use well-known payment methods such as bank transfer, credit card, online banking, PayPal, and more. The account can be capitalized in real-time, and you can start trading directly. Before the deposit, the mind must be fully verified. The broker will explain all the necessary steps for you.

Many brokers do not require a minimum deposit or just a small one of 100-200$ for the real money account opening. Among other things, position sizes can be chosen so that only a little money is risked.

Take advantage of toll-free deposits and withdrawals:

- Real-time deposits using electronic methods

- The majority of brokers require no fees

- Deposits even with very little capital

- Payouts will be sent within 1-3 days

- Bank transfer, PayPal, credit card, online banking, and other methods

4. Safeguard risk to make sustainable money

Let's talk about the most crucial topic for the trader. The risk of a trading transaction must be calculated precisely. It is always determined by the position size and the associated stop loss. I always recommend a trader to work with a stop loss. It is an automatic loss limit. They thus limit the possible damage.

How Much Money Should You Invest Per Trade?

Professional fund managers and traders use 1 - 2% of the total capital per position. The risk can also vary according to preferences. In the end, the dealer always decides himself which risk he wants to take. Sound risk management of 1 - 2% of the total capital is a perfect choice because several loss levels in a row will not burden the account extremely.

A trader will always have fluctuations in his performance. To be 100% correct is not possible. You still trade only with probabilities, and losses are part of it. It is also essential that you are not discouraged by failures but continue to follow his concept.

Use these tools for risk management:

- **Stop Loss:** Automatic loss limit that automatically closes the position at a specific price/loss.

- **Take Profit:** Automatic profit limit, which automatically closes the position at a guaranteed price/profit.

- **Position calculator:** Offered by the broker or integrated into the trading platform.

- Thus, you can optimally determine your position size and adjust the Money management.

- **Meaningful Money Management:** The portfolio

should be balanced. Too high a position can mean a quick stop for the account. Professionals use risk management of 1 - 2% of the total account per position.

Gain hedging with the stop loss

The stop loss also allows you to hedge profits or money. If a position is in the advantage and you want to secure a partial profit, you can follow the stop loss at any price.

5. Create trading rules and strategy

Now you have to think about which trading approach you want to pursue. There are countless trading strategies for the markets. This includes a proper analysis and the attention of relevant market news. The demo account is perfect for trying different methods.

The trading rules reflect the approach of a trader in the market. From my experience, it works very well if the dealer sets his own rules or others and strictly adheres to it. Emotional action must be hidden. Trading is like a job that has to be done step by step. That is why it is indispensable for me to trade without a set of rules.

The typical process of a trade:

- Fundamental analysis (news)

- Technical report (chart)

- Risk calculation

- Position opening

Further education and knowledge

Continuous learning is the way to success. Never deny yourself new information in trading because it could help you earn money. Many brokers offer a solid background in trading. The knowledge can then be extended by webinars or daily analyzes by professional traders. For the first profits, it is often sufficient to follow the strategies of a broker.

From my experience, I can say that simple strategies usually work best. Exchange trading does not necessarily have to be hard. It is a simple principle of supply and demand. Less is often more. That's why a clear set of rules is essential.

Never stand still and inform yourself in detail. Without learning, success, and success in trading will be missing.

How much money can you earn with trading?

Profits are unlimited in stock market trading. You can quickly get rich with speculation. The position size and risk play the most significant role here. The higher the risk, the higher the potential profit.

The most heavily traded markets are best for big money. Because these are the most liquid. This means that you always get the correct price execution because there is enough demand or supply available. To earn a lot of money, you also have to bring enough capital. The use of a lever allows the trader to make additional profits:

- Unlimited profits are possible

- "You need a lot of money for a lot of money."

- The bet always determines the possible profit.